OXFORD BOOKWORMS LIBRARY
Classics

Little Dorrit

CHARLES DICKENS

Stage 5 (1800 headwords)

Retold by Rowena Akinyemi
Illustrated by Chris Coady

Series Editor: Rachel Bladon
Founder Editors: Jennifer Bassett
and Tricia Hedge

OXFORD
UNIVERSITY PRESS

Great Clarendon Street, Oxford, OX2 6DP, United Kingdom

Oxford University Press is a department of the University of Oxford.
It furthers the University's objective of excellence in research, scholarship,
and education by publishing worldwide. Oxford is a registered trade
mark of Oxford University Press in the UK and in certain other countries

This simplified edition © Oxford University Press 2014

The moral rights of the author have been asserted

First published in Oxford Bookworms 2014

10 9 8 7 6 5 4 3 2 1

No unauthorized photocopying

All rights reserved. No part of this publication may be reproduced,
stored in a retrieval system, or transmitted, in any form or by any means,
without the prior permission in writing of Oxford University Press, or as
expressly permitted by law, by licence or under terms agreed with the
appropriate reprographics rights organization. Enquiries concerning
reproduction outside the scope of the above should be sent to the ELT
Rights Department, Oxford University Press, at the address above

You must not circulate this work in any other form and you must
impose this same condition on any acquirer

Links to third party websites are provided by Oxford in good faith and
for information only. Oxford disclaims any responsibility for the materials
contained in any third party website referenced in this work

ISBN: 978 0 19 423809 0

A complete recording of this Bookworms edition of
Little Dorrit is available on audio CD. ISBN: 978 0 19 423807 6

Printed in China

Word count (main text): 25,189 words

For more information on the Oxford Bookworms Library,
visit www.oup.com/elt/gradedreaders

ACKNOWLEDGEMENTS

*The publisher would like to thank the following for their permission
to reproduce photographs:* Alamy p.109 (Lordprice Collection);
Corbis p.111 (Hulton-Deutsch Collection).
Illustrations by: Chris Coady/NB Illustration

CONTENTS

Part 1: Poverty

1	Home	2
2	The Child of the Marshalsea	11
3	The Circumlocution Office	19
4	Little Dorrit's Admirer	27
5	Do Not Forget	33
6	The Marshalsea Wall is Down	41

Part 2: Riches

1	On the Road	48
2	A Letter from Little Dorrit	55
3	The Merdles	62
4	A Wounded Mind	68
5	Ruined	75
6	A New Prisoner	81
7	Unfinished Business	89
8	Sunshine and Shade	97

GLOSSARY	105
STORY NOTES	108
ABOUT VICTORIAN LONDON	109
ABOUT CHARLES DICKENS	111
ACTIVITIES: Before Reading	113
ACTIVITIES: While Reading	114
ACTIVITIES: After Reading	119
ABOUT THE BOOKWORMS LIBRARY	124

PEOPLE IN THIS STORY

Amy Dorrit (Little Dorrit)
William Dorrit her father
Fanny Dorrit her sister
Tip (Edward) Dorrit her brother
Frederick Dorrit her uncle

Arthur Clennam
Mrs Clennam Arthur's mother
Jeremiah Flintwinch Mrs Clennam's servant
Affery Flintwinch his wife, another servant

Mr Meagles Arthur's friend
Mrs Meagles his wife
Pet Meagles their daughter

Mr Chivery a jailer
Young John Chivery his son

Mr Tite Barnacle the head of the Circumlocution Office
Barnacle Junior his son

Mr Merdle a very rich businessman
Mrs Merdle his wife
Edmund Sparkler her son
Daniel Doyce an engineer and inventor
Mr Plornish a friend of the Dorrits
Mr Pancks a rent collector
Mr Casby a house owner at Bleeding-Heart Yard
Mr Rigaud a traveller

—PART ONE—
POVERTY

― CHAPTER ONE ―

Home

It was a hot August day, and the city of Marseille lay burning in the sun.

'We shall be out of quarantine today, Mr Meagles,' said Arthur Clennam, as the two men looked over the wall at the city in the distance.

'Out today!' repeated Mr Meagles. 'But what have we been in for?'

'For no very good reason, I must say,' said Arthur. 'But since we have come from the East, the health officials are afraid we might be sick.'

'I *am* sick now!' said Mr Meagles, but with a playful smile on his face. 'When I came here, I was as well as I have ever been in my life. But shut up here, I have been waking up, night after night, saying, "*Now* I am sick, *now* they will keep me here!"'

'Well, Mr Meagles, say no more about it, now it's over,' said a cheerful woman.

It was Mrs Meagles who spoke. Like her husband, she was healthy and bright, with a pleasant, homely English face.

Her daughter, close behind her, touched Mr Meagles on the shoulder, and Mr Meagles immediately forgave Marseille from the bottom of his heart. Pet was about twenty – a lovely girl, with long brown hair and wonderful eyes.

'Now, Pet, my dear,' said Mr Meagles, 'go with your mother and get ready for the boat. The health officials are coming to let us out at last.'

Arthur Clennam, a serious, dark man of forty, watched as

Mrs Meagles and Pet crossed the hot yard and disappeared through a white archway.

'Now, Mr Clennam,' said Mr Meagles, 'may I ask if you have decided where to go next?'

'I don't belong anywhere,' said Arthur. 'I was sent away to the other end of the world with my father before I was twenty, and kept there until his death a year ago. I have always worked at a job I hated. I am the only child of a hard father and a hard mother. Punishment and terror – nothing gentle anywhere – that was my childhood.'

The picture made Mr Meagles very uncomfortable. 'That was a difficult start,' he said. 'Now you must enjoy everything that lies beyond it.'

Arthur, with his serious smile, shook his head. 'Enough about me. Here is the boat!'

The boat was filled with officials, and as it landed, they came up the steps. All the travellers came together in the yard, and then names were called and papers were produced and signed. Finally, everything was done and the travellers were free to go.

'I always begin to forgive a place as soon as I have left it behind,' said Mr Meagles. 'I expect a prisoner begins to forgive a prison after he is let out.'

A few days later, Arthur Clennam, newly arrived from Marseilles, was walking through the streets of London. It was a Sunday evening, grey and tired. The rain began to fall, then umbrellas appeared, and wet skirts and mud. Arthur went down through the narrow streets, past silent buildings, until he came at last to the house he was looking for. An old brick house, so dark and dirty it was almost black, with long, narrow windows. Many years ago, the house had nearly slid down sideways, and it was now supported by huge wooden posts.

'Nothing changed,' said Arthur. 'Dark and miserable as ever.'

He went up to the door and knocked. There was a slow step on the stone floor inside, and the door was opened by an old man, bent and dried, but with sharp eyes.

'Ah, Mr Arthur?' he said, without any feeling. 'You are here at last? Come in.'

Arthur stepped in and shut the door.

'You've grown stronger,' said the old man, looking at him and shaking his head, 'but you aren't as fine-looking as your father, in my opinion. Nor your mother, either.'

'How is my mother, Mr Flintwinch?'

'Same as she always is now. Hasn't been out of her room fifteen times in fifteen years, Arthur.'

'Can I see her tonight?'

'Yes, Arthur, yes,' said Jeremiah Flintwinch.

Mr Flintwinch was a short, bald man, and his head and body were bent to one side. Just like the house, he too seemed to be sliding down sideways.

Arthur followed him upstairs, into a dark bedroom, where his mother sat on a black sofa, in widow's clothes. She gave him one glassy kiss, and touched his hand with her cold fingers. There was a fire in the fireplace, and the room was airless.

'Mother, this is not your old, busy life!'

'My world is now this narrow room, Arthur,' she replied. Her hard voice reminded Arthur of his frightened, cold childhood. 'I can't walk now. I haven't been outside this room for years.' She looked towards one corner of the room, where a chair on wheels stood in front of a desk. 'But I am able to carry out my business duties. I am glad of that. It is a bad night. Is it snowing?'

'Snow, Mother? It is only September!'

'All seasons are the same to me,' she said. 'I know nothing of summer and winter, shut up here.' On her little table lay two or three books, a pair of glasses, and an old gold watch.

'I see that you received the watch I sent you,' said Arthur. 'My father was very worried about it. He wanted me to send it to you as soon as possible. But he only told me about it just before he died.'

'No talk about business today,' said Mrs Clennam. 'Affery, it is nine o'clock.'

An old woman came forward from a dark corner of the room, and Arthur saw that there was a young girl sitting there, too. He did not know the girl, but he remembered the woman well. It was Mrs Affery Flintwinch, his mother's old servant. Affery brought a plate of bread and butter, and a glass of hot water and sugar. Mrs Clennam ate her supper and then read aloud from her book for a few minutes. As she read, the years fell away from her son, and all the dark horrors of his childhood bedtimes seemed to swallow him up. She shut the book and was still for a time.

'Good night, Arthur,' she said. He touched her hand and left the room.

Affery collected sheets and blankets and Arthur carried them upstairs to the top of the house. Up and up they climbed, through the airless smell of the old house, to a large bedroom. It was full of ugly, broken old furniture: old chairs, an old table, and an old bed. Arthur opened the long, low window and looked out at the forest of chimneys, and the red sky.

'All seasons are the same to me. I know nothing of summer and winter, shut up here.'

'She's awful hard, your mother,' Affery said. 'And he's a hard one, too, my husband Mr Flintwinch. He tells her what he thinks sometimes. It makes me shake from head to foot when I hear him talk to her like that. Don't you be afraid of them like me, Arthur.'

'Affery, who was that girl in my mother's room just now?' said Arthur.

'Girl?' said Affery, sharply.

'Yes, there was a girl, I saw her near you – she was almost hidden in the dark corner.'

'Oh! Her? Little Dorrit? *She's* nothing. Oh, Mr Flintwinch is coming!'

At the sound of footsteps on the stairs, Affery moved quickly away to the other end of the room. She was a tall, strong-looking woman, but before her sharp-eyed husband she was bent and fearful.

'Affery, woman, what are you doing?' Mr Flintwinch called through the door. 'Make Arthur's bed. Move yourself!'

At nine the next morning, Mrs Clennam sat in her chair on wheels. Old Mr Flintwinch pushed it across the room to her desk, and then he left the room in his sideways manner. Mrs Clennam opened a drawer in her desk. She took out some papers and began to read.

A little while later, Arthur knocked on the door. 'Good morning, Mother. Are you feeling better this morning?'

She shook her head. 'I shall never be better,' she replied.

'Can I talk to you about business, Mother?' Arthur asked.

'Your father has been dead for more than a year, Arthur. I have been waiting to speak to you ever since.'

'There was a lot to do before I could leave,' Arthur said. 'And when I did leave, I travelled a little, to rest. Mother, for some years now, our business has been less and less successful. I am sorry to cause you disappointment, but I have decided to leave. I have worked for the business for half my life, and I've never before done anything against your wishes. I ask you to remember that.'

Mrs Clennam waited. 'Have you finished, Arthur?'

'No, Mother, I have something more to say. It has been on my mind, night and day, for a long time. It is far more difficult to say than what I have said.'

Mrs Clennam took her hands from the desk and looked at the fire.

Arthur continued slowly. 'You were always stronger than my father. You sent him to China in order to take care of the business there, while you took care of it here. You decided that I would stay here with you until my twentieth year and then go to him.' He lowered his voice, and said with difficulty, 'I want to ask you, Mother, whether you ever suspected—'

At the word 'suspected', Mrs Clennam turned her eyes on her son with a fierce frown, and then looked back at the fire.

'—whether you suspected that there was some secret that caused trouble in Father's mind – that made him feel guilty?'

Again, Arthur paused, but his mother said nothing. 'Is it possible, Mother,' he whispered, putting his hand nervously on her desk, 'is it possible that Father had done something wrong to somebody?'

Arthur stopped, hoping that his mother would speak. Mrs Clennam looked at him angrily, but gave him no reply.

'Remember, Mother, I saw his face when he gave me the watch. He tried to write something to you, but he was too weak.

You can help me to discover the truth. Will you, Mother? If we owe money to anyone, let us find out and give the money back.'

Suddenly, Mrs Clennam turned and rang a bell on the wall. In a moment, Mr Flintwinch stood at the door.

'Flintwinch! Look at my son! He has only just arrived, and now he is accusing his father of wrongdoing. He suspects that our money is stolen money.' She was breathing quickly, but although she was terribly angry, her voice was low and clear. 'Yes, it's easy for you, Arthur, fresh from travelling the world and living a life of pleasure. But look at me, in prison in this room, in this chair! I have suffered without complaining for fifteen years!' She pointed at her son. 'Arthur, I tell you now, if you ever talk about this again, I will send you out through that doorway and never see you or know you again!'

Old Mr Flintwinch came across the room and stood beside Mrs Clennam. 'You suspect your own father, Arthur?' he said. 'You have no right to suspect him of any wrongdoing.'

'My son is leaving the business, Jeremiah,' said Mrs Clennam. 'You will now be my partner in the business and we shall swim – or drown – with it.'

The old man looked at Arthur, his eyes shining. 'Thank you, Mrs Clennam. I will never leave you. And Affery will never leave you, either. Now, twelve o'clock. Time for your lunch.'

Mr Flintwinch rang the bell, and the girl Arthur had seen the night before appeared with Mrs Clennam's lunch. Arthur now had the chance to look at her. She was about twenty-two, wearing a plain, shabby dress. She was so little and shy that she looked like a child, but there was too much anxiety in her face for a young girl.

It was so dull and dark at Mrs Clennam's house that after a few days, Arthur told his mother that he was going to stay at a hotel nearby. For a fortnight, he came every day to go through business papers and books with his mother and her new business partner. He saw Little Dorrit every day, sitting in a corner, her head bent over her sewing, her hands working quickly and busily. She worked almost every day from eight o'clock in the morning until eight o'clock in the evening, and was given lunch in the middle of the day. Arthur noticed that she always wanted to eat alone. She said that she was too busy to eat in the kitchen with Mrs Flintwinch.

As he watched Little Dorrit day after day, Arthur became curious about her. He began to wonder if she was connected with his father's secret. He decided to find out about Little Dorrit, and learn more of her story.

— CHAPTER TWO —

The Child of the Marshalsea

Not far from London Bridge, behind high walls with fierce iron spikes on the top, stood the Marshalsea Prison. Twenty-three years before, Mr William Dorrit had passed through its gates for the first time when his business failed and he lost all his money. Most prisoners left the Marshalsea after a few months, but Mr Dorrit was unable to pay his debts, and lived year after year in the prison, until the other prisoners began to call him 'the Father of the Marshalsea'.

Mr Dorrit's wife, his daughter Fanny, and his son Tip had come to live in the prison with him, and his younger daughter, Amy, was born there. But when Amy was only eight years old, her mother died.

Fanny became a wild girl, and Tip lazy; he went from job to job, saying that he was tired of everything, and at last became a debtor at the prison himself. But something in Amy, patient and serious, made her want to be useful for the family. She knew well that her father, who was so broken that he was the Father of the Marshalsea, could be no father to his own children. And so she learned to sew and began to go out to work. This Child of the Marshalsea grew into a woman, with no friend to help her, and soon became the head of the fallen Dorrit family.

This, then, was the life of Amy, known to all as Little Dorrit, who was now going home from Mrs Clennam's house on a dull September evening, watched from a distance by Arthur

Clennam. She walked through the darkening streets and across London Bridge, then turned in through the heavy wooden gate of the Marshalsea.

Arthur stood in the street outside, and waited to ask someone what the place was. A few people had already walked past him, too busy to stop, when an old man came slowly along the street and stopped to go through the gate. He was dirtily and poorly dressed in an old coat, once blue, which reached to his ankles and buttoned to his chin. He wore a broken old hat over a confusion of grey hair; and his trousers were so long and loose, and his shoes so large, that he moved slowly along like an elephant.

'Excuse me, sir,' Arthur said. 'What is this place?'

The old man stopped and looked at Arthur with weak grey eyes.

'This place?' replied the old man. 'This is the Marshalsea.'

'The debtors' prison! Can anyone go in and visit the prisoners?'

'Anyone can go *in*,' said the old man, adding plainly, 'but not everyone can go *out*.'

'May I ask you one more question?' said Arthur. 'Do you know the name Dorrit here?'

'My name, sir,' replied the old man, most unexpectedly, 'is Dorrit.'

Arthur took off his hat. 'May I just say a few words? I was not expecting this at all. I have recently come home after many years abroad. I have seen at my mother's – Mrs Clennam's – a young woman working, who is spoken of only as Little Dorrit. I have felt sincerely interested in her, and have wanted very much to know something more about her. I saw her go in at that gate, not a minute before you came.'

'Then you must come with me,' said the old man, in a weak and trembling voice. 'The young woman whom you saw go in here is my brother's child, Amy. My brother is William Dorrit; I am Frederick. I am a musician at a theatre and I help my brother as much as I can.'

He went through the gate and across the yard, and Arthur walked with him.

'My brother,' said the old man, 'has been here many years. Please say nothing about my niece working for your mother.'

The night was now dark, and the prison lamps in the yard and the candles in the prison windows did not seem to make it lighter. A few people stood about, talking quietly, but most of the prisoners were inside.

Frederick Dorrit turned in at one of the doors, went up the stairs, and paused for a moment before opening a door on the second floor. At once, Arthur saw Little Dorrit, and at once he understood why she always ate her dinner alone at his mother's house. She had brought the meat home and was warming it over the fire for her father. Her father, wearing an old grey gown and a black cap, sat at the table waiting for his supper. There was a clean cloth on the table, with a knife, fork and spoon, salt, and a glass on it.

Little Dorrit looked up and her face turned pale.

'This gentleman is Mr Clennam, son of Amy's friend,' Frederick told his brother. 'He was at the gate and wanted to come and greet you.' He turned to Arthur. 'This is my brother William, sir.'

'I have great respect for your daughter,' said Arthur, unsure what to say. 'That is why I wanted to meet you.'

But Mr Dorrit accepted the visitor easily. 'Mr Clennam, you are welcome, sir. Please sit down.' His voice was soft but proud. 'I have welcomed many gentlemen to these walls. Perhaps my daughter Amy has mentioned that I am the Father of this place. You know, I am sure, that my daughter Amy was born here. A good girl, sir, a dear girl; for many years a comfort and support to me. Amy, my dear, put the dish on the table. Will you join me, sir?'

'Thank you,' said Arthur. 'Nothing for me.'

Arthur was astonished at the man's manner. He did not seem to think that talking so freely about the family history might make his daughter feel uncomfortable.

Little Dorrit filled her father's glass with water, put his supper on the table, and sat down beside him while he ate. The way she looked at her father, half proud of him, half ashamed of him, all loving, went deep into Arthur's heart.

'Everyone who comes to the Marshalsea visits me. As many as forty or fifty in a day,' said Mr Dorrit, anxiously pushing his knife and fork around his plate. 'You must know, Mr Clennam,' went on the Father of the Marshalsea, 'that sometimes people who come here offer a little – something – to the Father of the place.'

Little Dorrit looked down, and put her hand anxiously on her father's arm. Mr Dorrit's voice was still soft, but it became more hesitant. 'It is generally – ha – money. And it is – it is often – hem – acceptable. Yes, very acceptable. Only last month, a gentleman visited me and offered me – ahem – two guineas.'

Arthur was wondering what to say when a bell began to ring and footsteps came up to the door. A pretty woman and a young man stood there.

'Mr Clennam, this is Fanny, my older daughter, and my son, Tip,' said Mr Dorrit. 'The bell is a signal for visitors to leave the prison, and so they have come to say good night.'

'Everyone who comes to the Marshalsea visits me,' said Mr Dorrit.

'I only want my clean dress from Amy,' said Fanny.

'And I want my clothes,' said Tip.

Little Dorrit opened a drawer and brought out two little piles of clothes, which she gave to her brother and sister.

'Mended?' Arthur heard the sister ask in a whisper.

'Yes,' answered Little Dorrit.

While they were talking, Arthur stood up and looked around the room. Although it was small and poorly furnished, it was neat and even comfortable. Everything in it was shabby but clean.

The bell went on ringing, and Fanny hurried out of the room. 'Now, Mr Clennam,' said Frederick as he followed her, 'we must go quickly, sir, or we will be locked inside.'

Little Dorrit had left the room after the others, and Arthur now turned to the Father of the Marshalsea and put something into his hand.

'Mr Clennam,' said the Father. 'I am deeply, deeply—'

But Arthur had gone downstairs with great speed. He saw Little Dorrit by the gate.

'Please forgive me,' he said, 'for speaking to you here. Please forgive me for coming here at all! I followed you tonight because I want to help you and your family in some way. I could not speak to you at my mother's house.'

Little Dorrit looked a little afraid. 'You are very good, sir. But I – I wish you hadn't followed me. Mrs Clennam has been very kind to give me work, and I don't want to have a secret from her.'

'Have you known my mother long?' asked Arthur.

'Two years, I think. We have a friend, Father and I – Mr Plornish. I wrote out notices which said that I was available for sewing work, and Mr Plornish gave them to people for me. That's how your mother found me. She doesn't know that I live in the prison.'

Little Dorrit was trembling and anxious. The bell stopped ringing. 'You must go, sir. The gate will be locked!' And she turned away to go back to her father.

That night, as Arthur tried to sleep, he wondered if his mother had a reason for helping Little Dorrit. Perhaps something she or his father had done had made William Dorrit fall so low. Was this the secret that had made his father feel guilty?

The next day, Arthur went again to the Marshalsea Prison and walked up and down outside the tall walls, waiting for the gate to open. Little Dorrit soon appeared, in her usual plain dress and with her usual shy manner.

'Will you allow me to walk with you this morning?' asked Arthur. 'I can speak to you as we walk.'

Little Dorrit looked anxious, but said, 'If you wish.'

The morning was windy, and the streets were miserably muddy, but no rain fell as they walked. Little Dorrit seemed so young in Arthur's eyes that at times he thought of her almost as a child.

'You spoke so sincerely last night, sir, and I found afterwards that you had been so generous to my father. I want to thank you, and I want to say to you...' She hesitated and trembled, and tears rose in her eyes.

'To say to me...?'

'That I hope you will not misunderstand my father. Don't judge him, sir, as you would judge others outside the gates. He has been there so long!'

'I will never judge him unfairly, believe me,' Arthur promised. 'May I ask you a little more about your father? Does he owe money to many people? Do you know who is the most important of his creditors?'

'I used to hear long ago of Mr Tite Barnacle,' Little Dorrit said, after some thought. 'He's very important in the Circumlocution Office.'

'It can do no harm,' thought Arthur, 'if I see this Mr Barnacle.'

'Ah!' said Little Dorrit, shaking her head. She seemed to

know what he was thinking. 'Many people used to think once of getting my poor father out, but you don't know how hopeless it is. And if he did get out, where could he live, and how could he live? He might not be strong enough for life outside the Marshalsea.'

Little Dorrit could not stop her tears, full of love and kindness, from falling. 'He would hate to know that I earn a little money! Such a good, good father!'

Arthur waited for these sudden feelings to pass a little before he spoke. 'You would be glad if your brother were free?'

'Oh, very, very glad, sir!'

'Well, we will hope for him. You told me last night of a friend you have?'

'Yes, sir, Mr Plornish. He lives in the last house at Bleeding-Heart Yard.'

Arthur took down the address, and gave his own address to Little Dorrit.

'Mr Plornish is one friend,' he said. 'And please believe that you have another friend now, too.'

'You are truly kind to me, sir.'

They walked back through the miserable, muddy streets, past crowds of dirty, shabby people. There was nothing pleasant about it at all. But to Arthur, it seemed a special walk, with that thin, careful little creature beside him.

— CHAPTER THREE —

The Circumlocution Office

The Circumlocution Office was the most important department in the government. Whatever needed doing, the Circumlocution Office knew best *how not to do it!* All the business of the country went into the Circumlocution Office – but most business never came out.

A few days after his conversation with Little Dorrit, Arthur found himself at the Circumlocution Office for the fifth time that week, asking for Mr Tite Barnacle. Mr Tite Barnacle was the head of this great office. Arthur had already spent one morning waiting for Mr Barnacle in a hallway, one in a waiting room, one in a small office, and one in a cold passage. On the fifth day, Mr Tite Barnacle was not busy; this time, he was absent. However, his son, Barnacle Junior, was available.

The young gentleman was standing in front of the fire in his father's office. It was a comfortable room, with a thick carpet and a leather-covered desk.

'Oh, I say! Look here! My father won't be in today,' said Barnacle Junior. He was a thin, young man with a little beard. 'Is there anything I can do?'

'Thank you,' said Arthur. 'I met a debtor in the Marshalsea Prison: Mr Dorrit. He has been there many years, and I wish to help him, if possible. I want to ask your father if he is one of Mr Dorrit's creditors.'

'I say! You must apply to the proper office here,' said Barnacle Junior.

'Tell me the proper office and I will go there,' said Arthur.

Arthur was sent from one office to the next, and finally given a pile of papers to take away with him. He took the papers miserably and walked slowly down the long stone passage that led out of the Circumlocution Office.

As he went through the building's front doors, Arthur was surprised to see Mr Meagles walking out in front of him. He was talking angrily to a friend.

'Mr Clennam!' said Mr Meagles when he saw Arthur, and his face slowly became more cheerful. 'I am glad to see you.'

'I am pleased to see you, too. How is Mrs Meagles? And your daughter?'

'They are as well as possible. I only wish you had found me in a better temper. Come and take a walk in the park with us, and I will tell you about this friend of mine. He is Daniel Doyce, an engineer and an inventor.'

The man was short and square, with grey hair and deep lines in his face.

'Twelve years ago, Daniel created an invention that could be very important to this country. He went to the Circumlocution Office to tell them about it – and they laughed at him, and sent him from one department to another. No one there understands how important it is. He was made to feel like someone who has done something wrong!'

'I am not surprised, after my own experiences at the Circumlocution Office,' said Arthur.

Doyce smiled. 'I should not have come here at all. I know of a hundred other people who have had the same experience, and I ought to have realized that this would happen. But I am very grateful to Mr Meagles here. He has supported me many times, in many ways.'

Mr Meagles was walking out in front of Arthur, talking angrily to a friend.

'Nonsense!' said Mr Meagles, whose temper had begun to cool a little. 'Now come, come! We won't make things better by feeling annoyed. Let's go back to your factory, Doyce. Mr Clennam, will you come with us to Bleeding-Heart Yard?'

'Bleeding-Heart Yard!' said Arthur. 'I want to go there myself, in fact.'

'Even better, then,' said Mr Meagles. 'Come along!'

And so the three of them walked through the shabby streets to Bleeding-Heart Yard. The Yard was reached by going down some steps. At one end of the yard stood Doyce's factory, and at the other end there were some tall chimneys, and big houses. The houses had once been grand, but were now divided up as homes for poor people.

Arthur looked around for the home of Mr Plornish, and saw the name on a sign above a gateway. It was the last house in the yard, as Little Dorrit had described it. Arthur said goodbye to Doyce and Meagles, and knocked at Mr Plornish's house. A fresh-faced, sandy-haired man of about thirty opened the door.

'Mr Plornish, I have come to talk to you about the Dorrit family,' said Arthur. 'Miss Dorrit told me you helped her.'

'Mr Clennam, is it?' said Mr Plornish. 'Yes, she's talked about you. Come in, sir.'

Mr Plornish led the way into a small, dark front room, and when they were sitting down, Arthur began to speak. 'I know that Miss Dorrit's brother is now a prisoner in the Marshalsea. I would like to pay his debts so that he can be released, but I want this to be a secret. Could you arrange it for me, and tell him that his debt has been paid by someone that you cannot name? Say that it is a friend who hopes that for his sister, if for no one else, he will use his freedom wisely.'

'I shall do just as you have asked, sir.'

'And if you can think how I could be useful to Miss Dorrit, in any way, I would be very grateful to you.'

'It will be a pleasure, sir,' said Mr Plornish. And, since Mr Plornish was eager to arrange things as quickly as possible, they then rode in a coach together towards the Marshalsea Prison, where Arthur left him before returning home.

After he had spent several more days at the Circumlocution Office, Arthur Clennam realized that William Dorrit's case was indeed a hopeless one. There was no way he could see of helping the Father of the Marshalsea to freedom. He thought about this one evening as he sat in his hotel in Covent Garden. Then he began to think about his own life, and all he had missed. He had a warm and sympathetic heart, and he felt sad to think about his life of loneliness.

'An unhappy childhood; long, lonely years abroad; and now home to England,' he said sadly to himself. 'What have I found?'

Just then, there was a gentle knock at his door, and it opened softly. A voice said quietly, 'Mr Clennam, it is me, Little Dorrit.' The words seemed to answer his question.

Arthur stood up and looked at her with his serious smile. 'My poor child! It is late and I have no fire – and it is so cold.' He made her sit in the chair nearest the fire, then brought wood and heaped it on. Soon, the fire was burning bright.

'I always think of you as Little Dorrit,' said Arthur. 'May I call you that?'

'Thank you, sir. I like it better than any name,' she said. 'I have come to tell you, sir, that my brother is free. Mr Plornish says that I can never know who paid his debts, and never thank the generous gentleman.'

'He would probably need no thanks,' said Arthur. 'He would probably be thankful that he had been able to help Little Dorrit a little, because she deserves it so much.'

Little Dorrit was trembling. 'If I knew him, and I might, I would tell him that he is very, very kind. If I knew him, I would go on my knees to thank him.'

'There, there, Little Dorrit,' he said gently.

There was fruit and cake on the table, and Arthur moved it towards her.

'Thank you, but I am not hungry,' she said. 'There was another thing I wanted to say. You wrote my father a note, saying you are coming to visit him tomorrow. Please, Mr Clennam, don't let him ask for money. Don't give it to him. You will be able to think better of him, if you don't.'

Arthur saw tears shining in her anxious eyes. 'If that is what you wish,' he said.

'Thank you, sir! I decided I had to speak to you. Not because I am ashamed of him,' she added, drying her tears quickly, 'but because I know him better than anyone does, and love him, and am proud of him.'

And then, Little Dorrit was suddenly anxious to leave and return to her father.

One Saturday morning not long after this, Arthur set out for Twickenham, where Mr Meagles lived. Mr Meagles had invited Arthur to come and stay with him and his family for the night, and as the weather was fine and dry, Arthur decided to walk.

He had crossed Putney Heath when he noticed Daniel Doyce walking ahead of him.

'How do you do, Mr Doyce,' called Arthur, catching up with him. 'I'm glad to see you.'

'Ha! Mr Clennam!' said Doyce. 'I hope we're going to the same place?'

'Twickenham? I'm glad to hear it.'

They walked on together, and were soon deep in conversation. Doyce was a man of good sense and confidence, who combined new ideas with patience and hard work. He told Arthur that he had worked and studied with an engineer when he was a young man. He had had a job offer in France, and had gone from there to Germany and then to Russia, where he had done very well indeed. When he came home to London, he had worked successfully – until he went to the Circumlocution Office, hoping that they would be interested in his invention, and was sent away.

'Do you have a partner in your business, Mr Doyce?' Arthur asked.

'Not at the moment,' he replied. 'I had one when I first went into it, but he has been dead for some years now. I didn't want to find another partner for a while, but there's more to do now and I can't manage everything. I'm hoping to talk about it this weekend with my friend and protector Mr Meagles.'

The Meagles's home was a pretty brick house by the river, with handsome trees all around it in a beautiful garden. As soon as Doyce rang the bell at the gate, Mr Meagles came out, followed closely by Mrs Meagles and Pet.

'Here we are, you see,' said Mr Meagles, 'in our own home. Not like Marseille, eh? We are delighted to see you, Mr Clennam, delighted.'

'I have not had such a pleasant greeting since we last walked up and down looking at the Mediterranean,' said Arthur. Then, remembering what Little Dorrit had said to him in his own room, he added, 'Except once.'

Mr Meagles led the way into the house. 'Come! You've had a long walk. You'll be glad to get your boots off.'

The house was as pretty inside as it was outside; and perfectly well arranged and comfortable. The day passed pleasantly, and dinner that evening was very enjoyable indeed. They had so many places and people to talk about, and they were all so easy and cheerful together. After dinner, they had some games, and Pet played the piano, but when the others went up to their rooms, Arthur waited to speak to Mr Meagles.

'I've recently stopped working in my mother's business,' he told him, 'and now I wish to find a new job. As we walked here today, Mr Doyce mentioned that he's looking for a business partner and he's going to take your advice. If you think that I would be a suitable business partner, perhaps you would talk to him about it?'

'I like the idea!' said Mr Meagles cheerfully. 'I will investigate. You would need to guide him, you know. But you can be perfectly sure of one thing: Daniel Doyce is as honest as the sun. Now good night, and sleep well.'

And with that, the two men went up to their rooms.

— CHAPTER FOUR —

Little Dorrit's Admirer

In the Marshalsea Prison, someone was in love with Little Dorrit. Young John Chivery was the son of a jailer, and he had loved Little Dorrit since he was a boy. He was a small, gentle man, with weak legs and one eye bigger than the other, but he had a great heart. He hoped to be a jailer like his father one day, and he thought they could be happy together – he and the Child of the Marshalsea, behind the lock, with the world shut out.

John's father, Mr Chivery, knew about his son's love for Little Dorrit, and so he looked after Mr Dorrit very well. Whenever Mr Dorrit came into the jailers' room, Mr Chivery allowed Mr Dorrit to sit in his armchair and read his newspaper. The Father of the Marshalsea, of course, was too proud to see that a jailer's son was in love with his daughter. But he always gladly agreed to sit in Mr Chivery's chair, and he accepted the presents that Young John brought for him.

Young John knew that Little Dorrit liked to walk on the Iron Bridge not far from the Marshalsea. So one Sunday after dinner, he dressed himself neatly in his best clothes, and went to find her there. She was standing looking down at the river, deep in thought. Young John watched her for a long time, and then walked on until he came near her.

When he said, 'Miss Dorrit!' she was surprised, and fell back from him, with an expression in her face of fear, and something like dislike. It made his heart fall. She had often avoided him before, but Young John had hoped that that was because she was shy, or because she knew of his feelings for her. Now, that quick look had said, 'You! I would rather see anyone else on earth than you!'

Young John watched Little Dorrit for a long time, and then walked on until he came near her.

She said, in her soft little voice, 'Oh, Mr John, is it you?' But she felt what her face had shown, and he felt it; and they stood looking at one another, confused.

'Miss Dorrit, I know that your family is far above mine. I know that my position as the son of a jailer is very low, but I have for a long time – ages – wished to say something to you. May I say it? I didn't intend to upset you today. I would throw myself in the river if it would make you happy for a moment! So I can't say any more unless you allow me to speak.'

Little Dorrit was trembling. 'If you please, John,' she said quietly, 'if you please – no, don't say any more.'

'Never, Miss Dorrit?'

'No, if you please. Never. You are so generous, and I know I can trust you not to say any more to me.'

'You can trust me,' said Young John, bravely. He was miserable, but her word was more than a law to him.

'Thank you, John,' said Little Dorrit. 'I hope you will have a good wife one day, and be a happy man.'

As she said these words, poor Young John burst into tears.

'Oh, don't cry!' said Little Dorrit. 'Don't, don't. Goodbye.'

'Goodbye, Miss Dorrit!' And he turned away and went home through the back streets, his great hat pulled down over his eyes, and the black collar of his purple coat turned up around his neck.

That evening, the brothers, William and Frederick Dorrit, walked up and down together in the yard of the Marshalsea Prison. Frederick, the free man, looked bent, old, and weak, while William, the prisoner, stood tall, proud, and confident of his position – and for this alone, they were a sight to see.

'I wish you would smarten yourself up a little, Frederick,' said the Father of the Marshalsea. 'You don't look after yourself enough. You must come and walk in the yard with me more regularly.'

'Hah!' sighed the other. 'Yes, yes, yes.'

The prison visitors were leaving, as the evening darkened.

'Look at me, Frederick, as an example. At regular hours of the day I walk in the yard, read the newspaper, have visitors, and eat and drink. I have taught Amy that I must have my meals punctually, and Amy knows the importance of these arrangements. You know what a good girl she is.'

The brother sighed again. 'Yes, William. But I am not like you.'

'But you could be, my dear Frederick, if you tried.'

As usual on Sunday nights, prisoners were saying goodbye to their visitors; and here and there, in the dark, a poor woman, wife, or mother was crying with a new prisoner. Many years before, the Father of the Marshalsea himself had cried in the shadows of the yard with his own poor wife. But that was a long time ago, and now Mr Dorrit made it very clear that people should not come and visit if they were going to cry. This Sunday evening, Mr Dorrit went with his brother to the gate. When he saw them, Mr Chivery touched his hat a little impatiently.

'Young John was looking very smart today, Chivery,' said Mr Dorrit.

'I wish the boy didn't spend his money on clothes. It only brings him trouble,' said Mr Chivery crossly.

'How does it bring him trouble?' asked the Father.

'Never mind,' said Mr Chivery. 'Mr Frederick going out?'

Mr Dorrit watched Frederick walk slowly through the door

and down the steps. Then he turned and went across the yard again, past prisoners who had no coat, no shoes, and no hope, and up the stairs to his own poor, shabby room. There, the table was laid for his supper, and his old grey gown was ready by the fire. His daughter was waiting for him. He sat down, but as he stared into the fire he began to feel uneasy.

'Something is wrong with Chivery,' he said slowly, and his uneasiness grew as he spoke. 'He was not – ha! – not as helpful as usual tonight. It – hem! – it's a little thing, but it upsets me, my love.'

Little Dorrit put her arm around his shoulders, but she did not look in his face while he spoke.

'I – hem! – I think Chivery is offended about something. Why, Amy? He is usually so respectful, and tonight he was quite – quite rude. Other prisoners were there, too!' Mr Dorrit was moving his hands anxiously. 'I might die of hunger if I lose Chivery's support!'

For a little while there was a dead silence and stillness in the room. Mr Dorrit's supper was cooking on the fire, and Little Dorrit moved to put it on the table. They sat in their usual seats and began to eat. They did not look at each other, but Little Dorrit could feel her father's growing anxiety. He put down his knife and fork with a noise, bit at his bread angrily, and then at last pushed his plate away.

'What does it matter if I eat or not?' he asked, standing up. 'It doesn't matter if my life ends now, or next week, or next year. What am I worth to anyone? A poor prisoner, fed on kindness.'

As he rose, she held her hands up to him.

'Amy!' he went on, trembling violently and looking at her wildly. 'I wish you could see me as your mother saw me. I was young, I was good-looking, I was independent. I was, child! If you could see me in those days, you would be proud!'

'Dear Father.' She held his arm, and persuaded him to sit down again, but he went on in the same wild way.

'I do have some respect here. Go out and ask who is the most important person in the place. They'll say it's your father.' And he burst into tears of pity for himself, and at last let her put her arms around him. 'Oh Amy, my poor, motherless child! You would have married a gentleman, and we would have ridden our own horses, side by side. You would have loved me more, I know.'

'You are the dearest, kindest father,' said Little Dorrit. She comforted him with her loving words, and slowly he became quieter. She heated his supper again and was happy to see him eat and drink. She talked to him about the new shirts she was going to sew for him, and about the new shoes he needed. (He never once thought of *her* dress or *her* shoes.)

'My love, you have had a difficult, hard life here,' he said. 'No friends, no time for yourself, and many duties, I am afraid.'

'Don't think of that, dear,' she said. 'I never do.'

Little Dorrit never left her father all that night. She sat by the fire as he slept. When morning came, she went down the stairs and across the empty yard to her own room, high up in the roof. She opened the window and looked at the sky. She thought of the sun rising on rolling rivers and wide seas, on rich fields and great forests. And then she looked down into the prison, where her father had lived for twenty-three years. The spikes on the high gates had never looked so sharp and cruel, or the yard so small and dark.

— CHAPTER FIVE —

Do Not Forget

Mr Meagles came to see Arthur at nine o'clock one morning.

'I've talked to Doyce about his business,' he said cheerfully. 'He's delighted that you're interested in it, and wants you to know everything about it. He's gone out of town for a week, so that you can go through his books and papers freely. Then, you can decide if you want to become his partner.'

They went to Bleeding-Heart Yard that same morning, and Arthur began to look at Doyce's papers. It was clear that Doyce needed help in the office, but everything was clearly arranged and carefully noted down, and after three or four days, Arthur had learned everything he needed to know. He was able to discuss with Mr Meagles how much he should pay for half the business — and found that Doyce had suggested an even smaller figure. And so, when the engineer came back to town, they were able to quickly agree to become business partners.

'If I had looked high and low, Mr Clennam, I don't believe I would have found a better business partner,' said Doyce.

'And I say the same!' said Arthur.

So Arthur began his new life, working at Bleeding-Heart Yard — and within two months, he knew everything about the running of Doyce's business. Raising his eyes one day, he looked out of the glass front of his office, down at the yard. He was surprised to see a short, dark man going quickly from house to house, talking loudly. Then the man came across to Doyce's factory and climbed the stairs to Arthur's office, puffing and blowing like a little engine.

'My name's Pancks,' he said, with his hat pushed back on his ears. His black eyes were sharp and he was biting the fingers of his right hand. 'I collect the weekly rents from Bleeding-Heart Yard for Mr Casby. May I come in?'

Arthur nodded, and Mr Pancks took his hat off and came across the room.

'Mr Clennam,' he began, 'I want information, sir.'

'About this business?' asked Arthur.

'No,' said Pancks, 'about Dorrit.'

'This is a strange visit, Mr Pancks. It's extraordinary that you should come to me,' said Arthur, looking carefully at Pancks's face. It was dirty, but eager and quick.

'I've met a young lady sewing at Mr Casby's house. I believe that she also does some work for your mother.' Pancks paused to bite his fingers again. 'I have heard the name Dorrit before, and I want to find out about her family. I think I might be able to help them. I can't say any more than that for now.'

After a little thought, Arthur decided to tell Pancks about the Father of the Marshalsea and the long years he had spent in prison because he could not pay his debts. He told Pancks about his attempts to help Mr Dorrit, and about the Barnacles at the Circumlocution Office.

'Now, since I have told you as much as I know, could I please ask that you tell me anything you learn about the Dorrit family?' asked Arthur.

Pancks agreed. He stood a little while, looking at Arthur, biting his fingers, and obviously fixing in his mind everything he had been told. 'Now I must go. I have a few more rents to collect in the yard today.'

Little Dorrit had finished a long day's work in Mrs Clennam's room and was putting away all her sewing, neat and tidy, before going home. Pancks had been visiting, and Mrs Clennam watched Little Dorrit and then said, slowly and thoughtfully, 'What do you know about that man, Little Dorrit?'

'I don't know anything about him, madam,' she said. 'Only that I have seen him here a few times, and at Mr Casby's house, and he has spoken to me.'

'Why does he come here to see you?' Mrs Clennam asked.

'I don't know, madam,' said Little Dorrit.

Little Dorrit got up to go, but as she stopped by Mrs Clennam's chair to say good night, Mrs Clennam put out her hand and laid it on her arm. 'Tell me, Little Dorrit,' she said. 'Have you many friends?'

'Very few, madam.'

'I believe I was your friend when you had no other. Is that right?'

'Yes, madam. Many times, without the work you gave me, we would have had nothing,' said Little Dorrit.

'Has it been very difficult for you?' asked Mrs Clennam. She picked up her husband's watch, which always lay on her table, and turned it over and over in her hands, deep in thought.

'Sometimes it has been hard to live,' said Little Dorrit in her soft voice, 'but I think not harder than many people find it.'

'Well said!' replied Mrs Clennam quickly. 'You are a good, thoughtful girl.'

Affery had come into the room at that moment, and she was astonished to see Mrs Clennam put her hands on Little Dorrit's shoulders and gently kiss her on the forehead, with a gentleness which Affery had not thought Mrs Clennam could show.

'Now go, Little Dorrit,' said Mrs Clennam, 'or you will be late, poor child.'

Affery followed Little Dorrit downstairs to let her out, and stepped outside the open door. It was a rainy, thundery evening, and she watched the clouds flying fast across the sky. Affery was afraid of storms, but she also hated the house and its strange darkness, so she did not hurry back inside. She was deciding whether to go in or stay out when a violent rush of wind blew the door closed, shutting her out.

'What shall I do now?' cried Affery. 'Mrs Clennam's all alone inside, and can't come down to open it.'

She pulled her apron over her head to keep the rain off, and ran crying around in front of the house. She was bending down to look through the keyhole when she suddenly heard someone behind her. She screamed, and looked around. A tall man was standing there. He was dressed like a traveller, wearing a thick, long cloak, and a tall hat. He had a long nose and a black moustache. He laughed at Affery's sudden cry, and as he laughed, his moustache went up under his nose, and his nose came down over his moustache.

'Why are you frightened?' he said.

'The wind has blown the door shut and I can't get in!' cried Affery.

'Hah! Indeed!' said the gentleman. 'Do you know the name of Clennam around here?'

'Of course I do!' cried Affery. 'She's here in this house! And she's all alone in her room, and can't walk. And my husband's out, and can't help. What can I do now?'

The gentleman stood back and looked at the house. His eyes rested on the long, narrow window near the door. 'Now, madam, shall I open the door for you?'

Affery screamed, and looked around. A tall man was standing there.

'Yes, please, and do it at once,' cried Affery. 'She may be calling me at this very moment. And I'm going out of my mind thinking of it.'

'I'll make a suggestion, then. I've just arrived on the boat from France.' He showed Affery his cloak and his boots, which were very wet, and Affery noticed that he was shaking with cold. 'I wanted to see Mrs Clennam within office hours, but I am late because of the bad weather. I'll open the door, if you will make sure Mrs Clennam will see me tonight.'

Affery was glad to agree to this suggestion, and the gentleman took off his cloak and gave it to Affery. He ran to the house and jumped up, and in a minute, he had opened the window and climbed in. He had strange and frightening eyes, and Affery suddenly thought that if he went straight upstairs to murder Mrs Clennam, she could not prevent him. But after a moment, he appeared at the front door.

'Now, my dear madam,' the stranger said, as he took back his cloak. 'If you could... What ever is that noise?'

It was the strangest of sounds. A tremble, and a low, heavy noise, then the sound of something light falling.

'I don't know what it is,' said Affery fearfully, 'but I've heard it many times.'

The man's trembling lips had turned colourless as he listened, but at that moment, he and Affery heard a voice from behind them, and turned to see Mr Flintwinch arriving back at the house.

'What's happening here, Affery?' said the old man.

'My name is Rigaud,' said the visitor, 'and I need to see Mrs Clennam.'

'Mrs Clennam is my business partner,' Mr Flintwinch said. 'Come into my office.' He lit a candle and led the way, in his sideways manner, across the hall to his office.

'Have you not heard about me from Paris?' asked the visitor.

'We have heard nothing from Paris about a Mr Rigaud,' said Mr Flintwinch.

Rigaud took a letter from his pocket and gave it to Mr Flintwinch. It was an official letter, from a trusted agent in

Paris, which asked Mrs Clennam to pay Rigaud fifty pounds.

'Very good, sir,' said Mr Flintwinch. The man's air of confidence had already made him decide that he was a true gentleman.

'I should like to see Mrs Clennam tonight for a few minutes,' said Rigaud, his moustache going up and his nose coming down in that most terrible of smiles.

Affery took the letter upstairs to Mrs Clennam, and Mr Flintwinch lit two more candles while Rigaud waited. Then he took the visitor up to Mrs Clennam's room.

'I apologize for visiting you so late at night,' said Rigaud.

'You are English, sir?' asked Mrs Clennam.

'No, no. I have no country. I have travelled in many countries, here, there, and everywhere!' the visitor said.

Mr Flintwinch made tea, and Mr Rigaud, in his most gentlemanly manner, got up and took a cup to Mrs Clennam. As he put the cup on her table, he noticed the watch lying in front of her as it always did.

'Excuse me for noticing it, but that's a very beautiful watch. May I?' he said, taking it in his hand. 'A gentleman's watch. I have often seen these in Holland and Belgium. Now, are these the letters D.N.F? They are difficult to read.'

'Those are the letters,' said Mrs Clennam.

'D.N.F. was some lovely, interesting creature, I'm sure,' said Mr Rigaud.

'The letters are not the first letters of any name,' said Mrs Clennam, coldly. 'They stand, I believe, for Do Not Forget!'

'And naturally,' said Mr Rigaud, putting the watch back on the table and sitting down again, 'you do *not* forget.'

'No, sir, I do not forget,' replied Mrs Clennam in her strong, deliberate voice. 'One does not forget, living a life as dull as mine has been these years. I neither forget nor wish to forget.'

She put her hand on the watch and moved it to the exact place on her little table where it always sat. Mr Rigaud listened to her, thoughtfully touching his moustache.

'Mr Flintwinch will give you your fifty pounds tomorrow. I hope your stay in this city will be pleasant,' said Mrs Clennam, with her frozen smile.

Mr Rigaud stood up to say goodbye, and followed Mr Flintwinch out of the room. He looked in all the rooms with interest, as he walked through the house.

'I love an old house,' he said, putting his long cloak on. He stopped to look at a painting on the wall. 'Who is this, Mr Flintwinch?'

'Mr Clennam. Her husband, now dead.'

'The owner of the watch?'

'Yes, Mr Rigaud.'

'They must have been very happy.'

'I can't say. I don't know,' said Mr Flintwinch. 'There are secrets in all families.'

'Secrets? So there are! You are right,' cried Mr Rigaud. And he threw back his head and burst into laughter.

'You will collect your money tomorrow, sir,' said Mr Flintwinch, politely.

'My dear sir!' Rigaud took Mr Flintwinch by the collar with both hands. 'I will collect my money, you have the word of a gentleman. You shall see me again!'

But Mr Rigaud did not appear the next day. Mr Flintwinch went to look for him at the hotel where he had been staying, and found that he had paid his bill early that morning and gone back to France. But Mr Flintwinch had a feeling that Mr Rigaud would keep his promise, and would return.

— CHAPTER SIX —

The Marshalsea Wall is Down

One morning, Pancks arrived at Arthur's rooms very early, when he was still in bed.

'I think I have made a discovery,' said Pancks, taking a packet of papers from his pocket. He turned the pages feverishly, and then held one out to Arthur.

'There, sir!' he cried, pointing at it. 'That man's your Father of the Marshalsea! He is heir to a great fortune, which has been waiting for him untouched for many years. He inherited a great house with land that had once been owned by the Dorrits of Dorset. Mr Dorrit just needs to sign a few papers, and he will be free – and extremely rich!'

'How have you discovered this?' asked Arthur in astonishment.

'When I first heard the name Dorrit, it meant something to me,' said Pancks. 'So I started to visit Mr Dorrit in the Marshalsea. When I learned about his family history, I was then able to make my own investigations.'

'Do the Dorrits know anything about this?' asked Arthur, smiling and shaking Pancks's hand.

'Not yet. I have only today heard from the bank and the lawyers,' said Pancks, biting his fingers. 'But Miss Amy Dorrit will be working at Mr Casby's house this morning, and I can now permit you to bring this news to the family in the way you think best. The sooner the better.'

Arthur, of course, decided to go at once to Mr Casby's house, and he was shown upstairs by a servant to the small room where Little Dorrit was sewing. When she saw the look on his face, she dropped her work.

'Mr Clennam! What's the matter?' she cried.

'I have come to tell you something: a piece of great fortune.'

They stood at the window, and her eyes, full of light, were fixed on his face. 'Dear Little Dorrit! Your father can be free within this week. We must go and tell him.'

Little Dorrit's face was pale, and her heart was beating fast.

'Shall I tell you more?' said Arthur, gently. 'Your father will be a rich man. You are all now very wealthy. Bravest and best of children, my dear Little Dorrit, you are now rewarded.'

'Father! Father!' was all she could say, before her eyes closed and she fainted onto the sofa.

Mr Casby's servants came and took care of her, but her concern to get to her father and to bring the news to him made her very quickly well again.

And so Little Dorrit came out of the house with Arthur and went in a coach to the Marshalsea. It was a strangely unreal ride through the old dirty streets and across the bridge. She felt that she was rising out of them into a world of wealth. Arthur told her that her father would ride in his own coach, a great and grand man, and she cried tears of happiness and innocent pride.

When Little Dorrit opened the door to her father's room, he was sitting in his old grey gown, reading his newspaper in the sunlight by the window. He turned around, surprised to see Little Dorrit was home, and surprised again to see Arthur Clennam. As they came in, the look on both their faces made his heart beat faster. He did not get up or speak, but quietly put down his glasses and newspaper on the table beside him.

Little Dorrit sat down close to him. 'Father! I've been made so happy this morning. Mr Clennam brought me such wonderful news about you.' Tears rolled down her face.

It was a strangely unreal ride through the old, dirty streets.

Mr Dorrit put his hand to his heart, and looked at Arthur. 'Mr Clennam? What surprise is waiting for me?'

'Tell me the best surprise you can imagine,' said Arthur.

As Arthur watched him, Mr Dorrit seemed to change into a very old man. The sun was bright on the wall outside and on the spikes along the top.

Silently, Mr Dorrit pointed at the wall.

'The wall is down,' said Arthur. 'Gone! Mr Dorrit, within a few days you will be free, and very wealthy. I congratulate you with all my heart on this change of fortune and the happy future ahead of you, into which you will carry your daughter – the best of all riches.'

Mr Dorrit began to shake, and Little Dorrit put her arms around him. 'I shall see you as my poor mother saw you long ago!' she told him. 'My dear, dear father.'

But Mr Dorrit could say nothing. Arthur and Little Dorrit helped him into a comfortable chair and brought him a drink. Then, as Arthur explained to him how Pancks had discovered the Dorrits' fortune, the Father of the Marshalsea sat back in his chair and cried.

After a while, he stood up and began to move around the room. 'He shall be – ha – Mr Pancks shall be generously rewarded, Mr Clennam,' said the Father. 'Everyone shall be – ha – rewarded and repaid. I will pay you, my dear sir, everything you have given me and my son. Chivery shall be rewarded. Young John shall be rewarded.'

He stopped for a moment to kiss Little Dorrit. 'We must send for Fanny and Tip. And for my brother.'

Little Dorrit was deeply anxious that her father should lie down and calm himself, but for another half hour he could only walk around the room, talking. At last, he lay down and slowly fell asleep, tears on his face. Little Dorrit had been sitting by his side, and now, exhausted by her own feelings, she dropped her head on his bed and fell asleep, too. Arthur got up quietly, left the prison, and went out into the noisy streets.

The next few days were busy. Mr Dorrit met his lawyers, signed all the papers, and complained greatly about the delay in his departure from the Marshalsea. Many prisoners asked Mr Dorrit for a few pounds, and he gave generously, although he always wrote first asking them to come and see him in his room. He gave them a great deal of advice, and hoped that they would remember the Father of the Marshalsea with respect.

Although Frederick Dorrit showed little interest in the family's changed fortune, Mr William Dorrit arranged for him to be measured for smart new clothes, hats, and boots; and ordered Mr Chivery to burn Frederick's old clothes. Fanny and Tip moved into the best hotel in the area, but complained that the best was very indifferent.

At last, the day arrived when Mr Dorrit and his family were to leave the prison for ever. As the clocks struck twelve o'clock, a coach was waiting at the gate. Not one of the prisoners stayed indoors; not one of the jailers was absent. All were wearing their best clothes. Near the gate stood Pancks, and Young John, with his broken heart.

'My dear Frederick,' said Mr Dorrit to his brother, as they left the room for the last time, 'give me your arm. I think we should go out together. And if you could throw a little brightness on your usual manner—'

'William, William,' said Frederick, shaking his head, 'you do all that. I don't know how. All forgotten!'

'But my dear Frederick, your position as my brother is now a fine one, and you must try to behave proudly.'

The brothers walked down the stairs and into the yard, and Mr Edward Dorrit (once known as Tip) and Miss Dorrit (once known as Fanny) followed them in their smart, new clothes.

There were three cheers as the Father of the Marshalsea went through the gate, and before the noise had died away, the family had climbed up into the coach that was waiting outside. Then, and not before—

'Goodness!' cried Miss Fanny. 'Where's Amy?'

They had expected to find her, as they always had done, quietly in the right place at the right moment. This going away was, perhaps, the very first thing in their family life that they had managed to do without her.

Miss Fanny looked out of the coach window into the prison, and her face turned red with anger. 'Now, I do say, Father,' she cried, 'this is too bad. That child Little Dorrit is being carried out in that ugly, old dress which I begged her to change. And by that Mr Clennam, too! She is making us all look foolish!'

Arthur appeared at the coach door, holding Little Dorrit in his arms. 'She has been forgotten,' he said, pity and blame in his voice. 'I ran up to her room and found that she had fainted on the floor, dear child. She was going to change her dress, and then it all became too much for her. Take care of this poor, cold girl, Miss Dorrit.'

'Thank you, sir,' replied Fanny, bursting into tears. 'Dear Amy, open your eyes, there's a love! Oh, Amy, I really am so annoyed and ashamed! Why are they not driving on? Please, Father, do tell them to drive on.'

The coach door was shut at last, and the Dorrit family drove away from the Marshalsea Prison.

—PART TWO—
RICHES

— CHAPTER ONE —

On the Road

It was autumn, and darkness and night were rising up the highest mountains of the Swiss Alps, and at last came to the walls of the great, old castle. A line of horses walked slowly up the steep, narrow path, led at the front by two guides who spoke to each other as they walked. There was no talking among the riders – two grey-haired gentlemen, two young ladies, and their brother – who were quietened by the sharp cold and the exhaustion of the journey. At last, they arrived at the castle door, and hurried into the building.

When they had seen their rooms, the Dorrit family came downstairs, where a bright fire shone red and high. A stranger was sitting near the fire, pulling at his black moustache. He had a long nose, and strange, frightening eyes.

'Are you on your way to Italy, sir?' the stranger asked Mr Dorrit.

'Yes,' Mr Dorrit replied. 'We are visiting the castle just for tonight, and return tomorrow to our hotel in Martigny. From there we continue to Italy.'

'Ah, yes,' said the stranger.

A servant came to tell them that dinner was ready, and the Dorrits moved through into the dining room. As they passed the stranger, Little Dorrit held her father's arm closely, trying to hide how much she trembled. With that high nose, and those eyes that were too near it, he was particularly disagreeable to her. He got up to follow them, and looked at the guest book, which lay open on the table.

There he read:

William Dorrit
Frederick Dorrit
Edward Dorrit   *From France to Italy.*
Miss Dorrit
Miss Amy Dorrit

Then, in small, complicated writing, he added his own name:

Rigaud, Paris

The sun was warm as the travellers came down slowly from the mountains and found themselves once more among the green fields, rocky rivers, and little wooden houses of the Swiss countryside. When they arrived at their hotel at Martigny, the hotel owner rushed out, hat in hand, apologizing endlessly. He wished he had not allowed it, he said, but a very important lady had begged him to let her and her son have their lunch in the Dorrits' rooms. They had promised to be very quick, and their coach was ready, but they had not yet gone.

Mr Dorrit's anger rose higher and higher as he heard these apologies. He felt that the family dignity had been attacked.

'A thousand apologies!' the hotel owner said again. 'Please do not be angry, sir. If you could possibly use another dining room for just five minutes...' the man begged.

'No, sir,' said Mr Dorrit, full of heat. 'I will not go into your hotel. I will leave without drinking or eating or stepping inside. You have insulted me! How dare you?'

At that moment, a man came out into the yard with a lady. 'My apologies,' said the rather heavy young gentleman. 'The lady – my mother – is extremely anxious to avoid an argument.'

The lady came forward. 'Edmund, I hope you are explaining that it is all my fault,' she said loudly. 'The hotel owner is not to blame!'

She walked slowly towards Mr Dorrit. 'I promised this man that we would be gone before you came back, but I had no idea that you would return so soon. I do apologize, and hope you will forgive the owner.'

The lady was Mrs Merdle, and her husband Mr Merdle was extraordinarily rich. He was in everything, from banking to building, and he turned all he touched to gold. All the best people in London – lawyers, doctors, politicians, government officials – wanted to know Mr Merdle. Mr Dorrit made a polite reply, and said that what he had first seen as an attack on his dignity, he now recognized as an honour. Hearing this, the lady smiled winningly.

'Are you on your way to Italy?' she asked.

'Yes, madam,' replied Mr Dorrit. 'We have just returned from a two-day excursion into the mountains, and from here we continue to Italy.'

'My son and I are also going to Italy,' said the lady. 'Perhaps we will have the pleasure of seeing you again there.'

Mrs Merdle's first husband had died a few years before, and Edmund Sparkler was her only son. He showed so little intelligence that some people said he had fallen out of a high window as a baby and landed on his head. He had asked any number of unsuitable young ladies to marry him, and was standing now staring at Miss Fanny Dorrit, as his mother tried to take his arm. She almost had to pull him into their coach, and he continued to stare back through the window until the coach disappeared.

As the family travelled on through Italy, Little Dorrit felt more and more that her present life was like a dream. All that she saw was new and wonderful, but it was not real. She felt that the pretty countries she saw from the window of the coach might disappear at any moment; and that, turning a corner, they might stop suddenly at the old Marshalsea gate.

They arrived at last in Venice, where they were to stay for some months in a palace on the Grand Canal. To Little Dorrit, Venice was more unreal than anywhere else, with its streets made of water, and the stillness of the days and nights that was broken only by the sound of bells and the cries of the gondoliers.

The family began a busy life, going here and there – but Little Dorrit asked only to be left alone. It was strange to have no work, no one to care for, nothing to plan. But strangest of all was the distance between her and her father. When she tried to take care of him, as she always used to, he reminded her that she was a lady now, who should behave with dignity. She often wanted to put her arms around his neck, and tell him how she loved him; but she knew that he would not like it, and that Fanny would be angry.

She spent a lot of time now with her uncle Frederick. He had begun to visit art galleries, and spent hours looking at the pictures, wiping his old blue nose. Little Dorrit had found him at a gallery one day, and after that she often joined him. He carried a chair for her, from picture to picture. He stood behind her, not speaking, but clearly happy to be with her.

Sometimes, Little Dorrit stepped into a gondola and went all over that strange city in her quiet, scared, lost manner. She looked into other gondolas, almost hoping to see the faces of the dear friends she loved.

Sometimes, Little Dorrit stepped into a gondola and went all over that strange city in her quiet, scared, lost manner.

But her favourite place was at the window of her own room, where in the evenings she watched the sun going down, purple and red, shining on the walls. She watched the stars appear, and she thought of the old prison.

The Dorrits had been in Venice for a month or two, when Mr Dorrit sent for his youngest daughter.

'Amy!' he began. 'I feel that you don't – ha! – seem at home here. Why is this?'

'I think, Father, I need a little time.'

'You disappoint me. I – ha, hum – am not pleased with you. You need to – hum – behave in the right way and do what someone in your position should.'

'I'm sorry that you have not been pleased with me, dear Father,' said Little Dorrit. 'I will try, more than ever, to fit into this new world around me.'

'You – ha – continue to hurt me. There are some past events which I wish – ha – to forget. You sister understands; your brother understands. Everyone understands – ha, hum – except you. You, Amy – hum – constantly remind me of the past. Though not in words.'

He looked down at Little Dorrit, who had put her hand on his arm. Her head was down, and he could not see her face, but her touch was soft and quiet, and there was only love in her sad little figure. He began to cry quietly, then said he was a hopeless old fool even with all this wealth, and took her in his arms. But his tears were soon dried.

With one remarkable exception, this was the only time, in his life of freedom and fortune, when he spoke to his daughter Little Dorrit of the old days.

Little Dorrit had been out with her sister one afternoon when, as they came back to the hotel by gondola, she noticed that another gondola was following them. Fanny opened the window near her, and watched as the other boat came up beside them.

'Did you ever see such a fool?' Fanny said, laughing.

'Who is it?' Little Dorrit asked.

'How slow you are!' said Fanny. 'Mr Sparkler, of course.'

Little Dorrit was silent for a moment, and then she asked, 'Are you going to encourage Mr Sparkler, Fanny?'

'I shall make him do what I want, my dear. I shall make him fetch and carry for me.'

'But dear Fanny, where do you think that will lead?'

'I haven't thought that far ahead yet,' said Fanny.

They climbed out of the gondola and walked up to the hotel, where Mr Sparkler joined them.

'Good day, Mr Sparkler,' said Fanny. 'I do hope your mother is well.'

'Thank you,' said Mr Sparkler hesitantly, 'she is very well.'

'Is she here in Venice?' asked Fanny.

'No, in Rome,' Mr Sparkler answered. 'I'm here by myself. I came to call on Mr Edward Dorrit. In fact, on the family.'

Turning politely to the hotel servants, Fanny asked whether her father and brother were in. Then, hearing that they were both at home, she took Mr Sparkler's arm and went with him upstairs to the Dorrits' grand rooms.

— CHAPTER TWO —

A Letter from Little Dorrit

Daniel Doyce had been asked to go and work abroad for a while, and before he went, Arthur went through the business papers with him.

'It's all in perfect order, Arthur. It couldn't be better.'

'Now, about the management of our money while you're away—' began Arthur.

His partner stopped him. 'You will continue in all matters to make decisions for both of us. I have perfect trust in you.'

With Doyce gone, Arthur's life had little variety. He worked every day at Bleeding-Heart Yard. Mr and Mrs Meagles had gone abroad themselves, travelling, and they had asked him to make sure their house was looked after while they were away. So visits to their house in Twickenham, and to his mother's home, were the only changes in his routine.

He sadly and sorely missed Little Dorrit. He had been prepared to miss her, but not so much. A large place in his life had been left empty when she went out of it, and he was lonely and felt suddenly that he was getting old. He had climbed a hill, gone over the top, and was going down quickly. He would always be alone, he could see: the day when he could fall in love was gone and would never shine again.

When he received a letter from Little Dorrit, he was greatly moved, but saw at once that her kind thoughts for him were now a secret from her family. The Dorrits had turned against him, as they had turned against everything from their prison days.

Dear Mr Clennam,

I write to you from my own room in Venice, hoping that you will be glad to hear from me.

We are all quite well. You will be pleased, I am sure, to know that my father's health is very good. He is very different indeed from what he used to be. Fanny, too, is much changed. She gets kinder every day, and is so patient. She has very quickly become used to our new fortunes: she is a natural lady. But I have not been able to, and sometimes I think I never will.

We have been in many wonderful places, and have seen many wonderful sights. But everything in my life is so strange, and I miss so much. I think all the time of home. I wish I knew – but I must ask you not to write to me – how Mr Plornish is. I love so dearly the place where I was poor, and where you were kind to me. Oh, so dearly!

And I must share one last thought with you: ever since I have been away, I have been afraid that you may think of me in a new light, or a new character. Please never think of me as the daughter of a rich person: remember me only as the shabby little girl you helped so kindly. I hope that you sometimes, in a quiet moment, have a thought for me.

Your ever grateful
Little Dorrit

Arthur had been working late a lot, and spending time in the waiting rooms of the Circumlocution Office, trying again to interest people in Doyce's invention. He was feeling tired and lonely, so on the day he received Little Dorrit's letter, he visited Mr Plornish, to give him her news, and then went to find Pancks, who was puffing and blowing in the yard.

Arthur went to find Pancks,
who was puffing and blowing in the yard.

'Come home with me and share my dinner,' said Arthur. 'I'm tired and miserable tonight. Mr Doyce has gone to work abroad, and I am quite alone.'

Pancks and Arthur had become friends since the Dorrits' departure from London, and they often talked of Little Dorrit and her goodness. The two men walked home to a dinner of bread and soup, served on a little table in front of the fire.

Mr Merdle's name was on Pancks's mind that evening.

'Merdle, Merdle. Everyone is talking about him. The wealthiest banker in the City,' said Pancks. 'I've looked into it. Putting money in Merdle's bank makes sense. It's a safe way to become rich.'

'Do you mean, my good Pancks, that you would put a thousand pounds of yours – say, the thousand pounds that Mr Dorrit paid you for discovering his inheritance – in Merdle's bank?' asked Arthur.

'Yes, indeed. I've already done it,' said Pancks, looking wisely at Arthur. 'Merdle is a man of enormous wealth. He has great influence with the government. His bank is safe.'

'Well!' said Arthur, looking at Pancks and then at the fire. 'You surprise me!'

'Don't say that, sir,' replied Pancks. 'It's what you ought to do yourself. Is it you who manages the money in your business with Daniel Doyce?'

'Yes, as well as I can.'

'Manage it better, sir. Reward him for his hard work and disappointments. You can make a lot of money if you put some into Merdle's bank. Go in and win!'

'But what if I go in and lose?' asked Arthur uneasily.

'You can't,' said Pancks. 'Merdle's name is everywhere.'

The two men spoke little more after this, but the next day

Arthur thought again and again about what Pancks had said. He thought how much he would enjoy making Doyce a little wealthier. He thought about how he saw or heard the name of Merdle everywhere. He began to think it was interesting, too, that everyone seemed to trust this man.

One evening a few weeks later, Arthur left his rooms at about nine o'clock and slowly walked in the direction of the cold home of his childhood. He had turned into the steep, narrow street when a man walked quickly up behind him and came past so close that Arthur was pushed against the wall.

Arthur arrived at his mother's house, and was surprised to see the same man there, looking up at his mother's window and laughing to himself. He was a strange man, with a high nose and a black moustache, and his eyes had a cruel, false expression. He wore a long, heavy cloak, and he looked like a man who was travelling. The man went up to the door and knocked at it.

'No! You again!' Affery cried out, as she unlocked the door.

'Me again, dear Mrs Flintwinch,' said the man. 'Open the door, beautiful Mrs Flintwinch. Let me go upstairs and see the lady. And fetch Mr Flintwinch; tell him that Rigaud has just arrived in England.'

The stranger walked inside, and Arthur, who had come up behind him, followed him into the house.

'Tell me, Affery,' said Arthur, looking angrily at Rigaud from head to foot, 'who is this gentleman?'

The voice of Mrs Clennam called from upstairs. 'Affery, let them both come up. Arthur, come straight to me!'

'Arthur!' said Rigaud, taking off his hat. 'The son?' His nose went down and his moustache went up, in an ugly smile.

Arthur did not answer. He went upstairs to his mother's room and Rigaud followed him.

'Madam,' said Rigaud, sitting down, 'perhaps you would introduce me to your son. It appears that I do not please him.'

'Sir,' said Arthur, 'whoever you are, if this were my house, I would not hesitate to put you outside it!'

'But it is not your house,' said his mother, without looking at him. 'The gentleman came here before,' she went on, 'with a letter from a trusted agent in Paris. I do not know why the gentleman has come again, but I'm sure he will explain, when Mr Flintwinch returns, and I'm sure it will be a simple business matter.'

'We shall see, madam,' said the man. As they talked, Arthur noticed that Mrs Clennam's manner and voice were under control, but that she never took her eyes off Rigaud's face, and listened carefully to every word he said.

Mr Flintwinch knocked at the door and came into the room, and Rigaud got up from his chair, laughing loudly. He wrapped his arms around the old man.

'Ah, Flintwinch!' he cried. 'How are you, my good little boy?' He clapped his hand hard on Mr Flintwinch's back, then pushed him roughly away and sat down again.

As Arthur watched in astonishment, his mother turned towards him.

'Please leave us to our business, Arthur,' she said. He bent down to kiss her, and Arthur felt that her face was even colder and harder than usual.

'Affery,' whispered Arthur, as he went downstairs into the dark hall. 'What's going on here? I want to know what is wrong. I want some light thrown on the secrets of this house.'

The old servant stood in the dark with her apron thrown over her head.

'Don't ask me anything, Arthur. There's noises in this house that frighten me. Noises, tremblings overhead, tremblings underneath.'

'But those are not all the secrets. I beg you to tell me more. Tell me about that foreign man, Rigaud.'

'The first time he came here, he heard the noises himself, and he was shaking,' said Affery.

'But what does he want, Affery?' said Arthur. 'What is the mystery that surrounds this house?'

'I don't know! Don't ask me anything, Arthur. Go away!' Arthur went out and Affery shut the door. As he looked up at the dark windows of his mother's room, they seemed to repeat, 'Don't ask me anything. Go away!'

— CHAPTER THREE —

The Merdles

From Venice, the Dorrits travelled on to Rome, and soon after they arrived there, they received a visit from Mrs Merdle.

'I'm delighted,' she said, 'to meet you once again, after our unfortunate misunderstanding at Martigny. And I must thank Mr Dorrit for making my son Edmund's stay in Venice so agreeable. I believe he was invited to your hotel several times.'

'I was pleased,' said Mr Dorrit, 'to show how greatly I – with the rest of the world – respect Mr Merdle's character. I have been – ha – disappointed to hear from Mr Sparkler that Mr Merdle has no plans to come abroad.'

'Why indeed,' said Mrs Merdle. 'He's so very busy, and wanted by so many people, I fear he cannot. He hasn't been able to get abroad for years.'

'I hope, however,' Mr Dorrit went on, 'that if I do not have the honour of meeting Mr Merdle on this side of the Alps, I shall have that honour when I return to England. I would be delighted to meet him.'

'Mr Merdle,' said Mrs Merdle, who had been looking admiringly at Fanny, 'will, I'm sure, be just as delighted.'

News soon spread in Rome that Mr Sparkler now had a position in the Circumlocution Office. The Barnacles, wanting to please Mr Merdle, had given young Sparkler a job. Mrs Merdle received congratulations from her friends in Rome. She hoped that Edmund would like the job, she said, but really she did not know. It would keep him in town a lot, and he preferred the country. But it was not a disagreeable position, and it was probably best that he should have something to do.

Miss Fanny was now in a difficult position. It was widely known that she was the lady whom Mr Sparkler admired. She could not decide whether to get rid of him or whether to encourage him more, and she came home one night anxious and upset from a party at Mrs Merdle's house, and went to Little Dorrit's room.

'Things cannot go on the way they are,' she cried, walking around the room.

'Sit down and let us talk,' said Little Dorrit. 'Tell me what you mean.'

'My dear,' said Fanny, kissing her, 'in spite of our money, we have disadvantages in this world. We are newcomers into fashionable life.'

'No one would see that in you, Fanny,' said Little Dorrit.

'My dear child,' said Fanny, 'it's most kind of you to say so. But although Father is very gentlemanly, he is in many small ways different from other gentlemen of his fortune. Uncle Frederick is completely unpresentable, and Edward spends far too much money, in a way that is giving him a bad name. Therefore, I find myself trying to decide whether I should carry the family through.'

'How?' asked her sister anxiously.

'The Merdles are a very good connection,' Fanny told Little Dorrit. 'Mr Sparkler has now got an excellent position. And although he is not clever, I doubt very much whether a clever husband would be suitable for me.'

'Oh, my dear Fanny!' A kind of terror was coming over Little Dorrit, as she began to understand her sister. 'You know that you have qualities to make you the wife of a much better man than Mr Sparkler. If you loved someone, Fanny, you would forget yourself.'

'Oh, indeed!' cried Fanny. 'Really? You know all about it, do you? Well, I won't marry Mr Sparkler tonight, my dear, or tomorrow morning. But I want a better position in society.' She began to walk around the room again.

'Things cannot go on the way they are,' Fanny cried.

'My dear sister,' said Little Dorrit, anxiously, 'would you give yourself an unhappy life, just to have a better position in society?'

'It wouldn't be an unhappy life, Amy. It's the life that I am fitted for.' She gave a short laugh. 'Don't argue with me. I understand these matters much better than you do. Now we have talked this over comfortably, we can go to bed. You dear little creature, good night!'

After this conversation, Little Dorrit watched Fanny's behaviour towards Mr Sparkler carefully. There were times when she became sharply impatient with him, and there were times when they got on much better, and when he amused her. He followed her through rough and smooth, like a small boat that is pulled through the water by a much larger ship.

One sunny afternoon, as Little Dorrit sat at the window, looking down at the street, Fanny came into the room, and sat next to her.

'Well, Amy dear, I am engaged to Mr Sparkler. We must tell Father tonight. Very little more needs to be said.'

The two sisters put their arms around each other and cried. It was the last time Fanny showed her feelings about the marriage. From that hour, the path she had chosen was before her and she walked it with her own proud step.

Mr Dorrit received the news of his daughter's engagement with great dignity. He told Fanny that he was proud of her; she was a child who was aware of the honour of the family name. Mr Dorrit expressed his delight that a family connection had been opened with Mr Merdle, the leading light of the age.

Fanny and Mr Sparkler were married in the spring, as Mr Sparkler's job at the Circumlocution Office was beginning soon. The night after their wedding, when the newly-married couple had left for a holiday in Florence, Little Dorrit sat in her room, feeling lonely. She wished that she could make her father's supper and sit by him, quietly sewing. But that could no longer happen. There was an Italian cook in the kitchen, and servants always nearby.

'Amy, my dear,' said Mr Dorrit, after supper, 'today has – ha – greatly pleased me. Your sister has made – hem – a very good marriage. My love, I hope soon a – ha – suitable partner will be found for you.'

'Oh no!' cried Little Dorrit, in alarm. 'I want to stay and take care of you always.'

'I have – hum – no gentleman in mind at present. But soon – ha – we must find you a suitable husband. Good night, my dear daughter.'

Mr Dorrit travelled with Mr and Mrs Sparkler from Florence to London. He took a room in a hotel in Brook Street, Grosvenor Square, and was having breakfast there one morning in his dressing gown when a servant came in and said that Mr Merdle had come to see him.

'Mr Merdle, this is – ha – thank you!' said Mr Dorrit, jumping up. He trembled to speak to the great man.

Mr Merdle was a quiet man, with a big head, and a rather uneasy expression on his dull, red face. He was silent for a while, then he finally said, 'I am glad to see you, sir.' He sat down, and passed his great hand over his exhausted head. 'I hope you will have dinner with me today – and every day during your stay in town.'

Mr Dorrit was delighted by the invitation. 'I am here only –

ha – a fortnight. To meet you – and to arrange – ha, hum – my fortune in the best way.'

'Well, sir,' said Mr Merdle, 'if I can be of any use to you, please ask me.'

'I did not dare – ha – to hope for your advice,' said Mr Dorrit. 'Though I would of course have followed it.'

'You know we are almost relations, sir,' said Mr Merdle, curiously interested in the pattern of the carpet, 'and, therefore, please consider me at your service.'

'Thank you!' cried Mr Dorrit. 'You are very good.'

'Of course, everything must be done honestly and properly.'

'Of course,' said Mr Dorrit. There was calm and silence in the room. Mr Merdle passed his hand again and again over his forehead.

'My time is rather precious,' said the great man, suddenly getting up. 'I must be moving toward the City. Can I take you anywhere, sir?'

As Mr Dorrit's bank was in the City, he accepted the invitation eagerly, and when he had dressed, he took Mr Merdle's arm and went down the stairs of the hotel and into the great man's coach. It was a wonderful dream to Mr Dorrit, to ride through the streets of London with the light of Mr Merdle shining around him. And then, when Mr Merdle got out and insisted that Mr Dorrit continue in his coach to the bank, Mr Dorrit heard everywhere, with the ears of his mind, 'Look at that wonderful man, Mr Merdle's friend!'

After that, dinner invitations to Mr Dorrit came every hour of the day. As the friend and relation by marriage of the famous Mr Merdle, everybody wanted to know him. Mr Dorrit felt more and more that this connection had brought him the position in society he deserved.

— CHAPTER FOUR —

A Wounded Mind

Mr Dorrit's time in London soon came to an end. After a last dinner at Mr Merdle's, he said goodbye to Fanny and was then led from the house to his coach by the great man himself. His heart was still full with pride from this final honour when he arrived at his hotel. He was walking through the hall with a calm sense of excellence when he saw something that stopped him dead: young John Chivery, in his best clothes, with his tall hat under his arm! Mr Dorrit stood, horrified, for a few moments.

'Ah! John!' he gasped at last, turning to the hotel servants. 'The young man may come up! Let him follow me.'

Young John followed Mr Dorrit to his rooms, smiling and pleased with his welcome. The servants lit the candles, and left the room.

When they were safely alone, Mr Dorrit turned around angrily towards John and caught hold of his collar. 'Now, sir. What do you mean by this? How dare you come here? How dare you insult me?'

Young John had expected Mr Dorrit to put his arms around him, and his face was a picture of astonishment and horror.

'I beg you to forgive me, sir,' said Young John, moving away towards the door.

'Stop, sir!' cried Mr Dorrit. 'Stop! Sit down!'

Young John dropped into the chair nearest the door, and Mr Dorrit walked up and down the room; rapidly at first, then more slowly. Then he turned and asked: 'Why did you come here?'

'Only to say, sir, that I hope you are well, and only to ask if

Miss Amy is well?'

'What's that to you?' asked Mr Dorrit.

'It's nothing to me, sir. I know there is a distance between us, I'm sure. I never thought you would take it badly,' said Young John, his voice trembling.

Mr Dorrit was ashamed. He went back to the window and stood there for a while with his forehead against the glass. When he turned at last, he looked tired and ill.

'John, I'm very sorry that I was angry with you, but – ha – some memories aren't happy, and – hum – you shouldn't have come. I would like to send a little – hum – something, with you, to be divided among – ha, hum – them. Will you take it?'

'There's many of them, I'm sure, who would be grateful.'

Mr Dorrit's hand shook, so it took him a long time to write a cheque for one hundred pounds.

'I hope you'll – ha – forget what has happened, John,' said Mr Dorrit, putting the cheque in John's hand.

'Don't speak of it, sir,' said John. But his words did not bring back the colour to Mr Dorrit's face.

'And John,' said Mr Dorrit, 'I hope that you won't say to anyone in the hotel that – hum – once I –'

'I promise you, sir,' said Young John. 'In my poor way, sir, I'm too proud and honourable to talk about those things.'

But Mr Dorrit was not too proud and honourable to listen at the door, to hear whether Young John went straight out or stayed to talk with anyone. There was no doubt that he left the hotel at once and went away down the street with a quick step. And Mr Dorrit was able to sit quietly alone, with his face to the fire.

The next morning's sun saw Mr Dorrit on the dusty Dover road, and the following day saw him at Calais. With the Channel between himself and Young John Chivery, he began to feel safe, and to find that the foreign air was lighter to breathe than the air of England.

It was late when Mr Dorrit's coach, on its last tired journey, arrived several days later at the hotel in Rome. Leaving the servants to unload the coach, Mr Dorrit went up the grand stairs slowly, feeling very tired, and looked into several rooms until he saw a light. As he stopped at the open door, he felt a pain in his heart. Surely it was not jealousy?

There were his brother and his daughter. Frederick was near the fire and Little Dorrit was sitting at a table, sewing. Mr Dorrit had sat many times, like his brother did now, in front of a fire far away, and she had sat with him. But surely there was nothing to feel jealous of in the memory of that old, miserable poverty?

'Do you know, Uncle, I think you're growing young again!' Little Dorrit was saying. 'So cheerful, and so interested in everything.'

'My dear child – all you. You have done me so much good, looking after me,' said her uncle. He looked up and saw Mr Dorrit standing in the doorway. 'Ah! Why, here's your father, Amy! My dear William, welcome back!'

With a cry of pleasure, Little Dorrit put her arms around her father and kissed him again and again.

Her father was a little impatient. 'It appears you were not – ha – expecting me. I began to think – ha, hum – to think I needed to apologize – ha – for returning.'

'Dear Father, you shall have supper in a very few minutes,' said Little Dorrit. 'You look tired.'

'You're wrong,' said Mr Dorrit, quickly. 'I'm not tired; I'm very much fresher than I was when I went to England!'

He was almost angry, so Little Dorrit said no more, but stayed quietly beside him, holding his arm. As Mr Dorrit stood like this, he fell into a heavy sleep for just a few moments, then woke suddenly.

'Frederick,' he said, turning on his brother. 'I recommend you to go to bed immediately. Ha. You should have been in bed long ago.'

'Well, well, I suppose I should,' said the old man. Mr Dorrit had fallen asleep again before his brother left the room. His supper was brought, and put on the table, and Little Dorrit sat at his side and poured out his drink for him, for the first time since they had left the Marshalsea. She was afraid to look at him much, but she noticed that twice he looked around him, and she thought that he almost seemed surprised that they were not in the old prison room. Both times, he put his hand to his head, and Little Dorrit thought that perhaps he was trying to feel the old black cap which he had always worn in the Marshalsea.

Over the next two days, Mr Dorrit fell asleep several times during meals. On the evening of the second day, he and Little Dorrit were both invited to Mrs Merdle's for dinner. Little Dorrit was dressed and ready before her father appeared, looking very old and thin, and she went with him with an anxious heart.

Mrs Merdle welcomed them with great honour. It was a grand dinner, with many important guests. The table was long, and the meal was long, and Little Dorrit lost sight of her father until a servant came to her with a note from Mrs Merdle.

'Please come and speak to Mr Dorrit,' the note read. 'He's not well.'

Little Dorrit was hurrying to her father when he got up out of his chair and called to her.

'Amy! Amy, my child!'

Immediately, conversation stopped and there was silence in the grand room.

'Amy,' he repeated. 'Please see if Chivery is at the gate. Of all the jailers, Chivery is a friend.'

'Dear Father, I am here,' said Little Dorrit, gently trying to move him away from the table.

'I can't get up the stairs without Chivery,' he said, annoyed.

All the guests were now talking in confusion, and everyone stood up. Mr Dorrit looked around him, and seeing so many faces, spoke to them.

'Ladies and gentlemen, it is my duty – ha – to welcome you to the Marshalsea. Welcome to the Marshalsea! Those who live here – ha – call me the Father of the Marshalsea. This is my child, ladies and gentlemen. My daughter, born here!'

Little Dorrit was not ashamed of him. She was pale and frightened, but she only wanted to calm him and get him away. Her quiet voice was heard gently begging him to leave the room with her.

Mrs Merdle, horrified, had managed to get the other guests out of the room, and Little Dorrit was left alone with her father.

'Come with me now, Father,' she said gently.

But no, he said he would never get up the stairs without Chivery. Where was Chivery? Would no one fetch Chivery?

'Let's go and look for Mr Chivery,' she suggested, and so she got him outside into a coach and home.

A Wounded Mind

'Amy,' Mr Dorrit repeated. 'Please see if Chivery
is at the gate. Of all the jailers, Chivery is a friend.'

Back at the hotel, Little Dorrit and Frederick took Mr Dorrit upstairs to his room and laid him down on his bed. His poor, wounded mind had forgotten the dream that it had been living since the discovery of the Dorrits' fortune, and it now knew of nothing except the Marshalsea.

The child who had done so much for him was never out of his mind. He loved Little Dorrit in his old way. They were in prison again, and she looked after him, and he needed her constantly. As for her, she bent over his bed with her quiet face against his, and would have laid down her life to make him better.

For ten days, Little Dorrit cared for him. Sometimes she was so exhausted that for a few minutes she would sleep with her head beside his. He became extremely weak, and then, quietly, quietly, he floated into rest.

Frederick and Little Dorrit, silent and sad together, stayed with the body until midnight, and then Little Dorrit took her uncle to his room and saw him lie down. She fell on her own bed, exhausted, and went into a deep sleep.

The moon rose late that night. When it was high in the sky, it shone through the window into the room where a life had just ended, and it shone not on one but on two quiet figures. Frederick Dorrit had gone back into the room and, kneeling on the floor, had bent his face over his brother's hand and there taken his last breath. Both brothers lay still, removed from the busy earth, and far beyond the judgements of this world; high above its mists and confusions.

— CHAPTER FIVE —

Ruined

Mr Edmund Sparkler and his wife Fanny were now living in their own house. It was a small, inconvenient house, but it was in a good area of London. Fanny, when she heard about the deaths of her father and uncle, had cried violently for twelve hours. Then she had got up to decide which new black dresses she was going to wear.

One hot summer evening, about three months later, Fanny lay on the sofa in her sitting room. She looked through the open window, over boxes of flowers, across the narrow street, at the open window of the house opposite. She was tired of that view. She looked at her husband, who was standing at the other window. She was tired of that view, too.

'If you have anything to say, Edmund, why don't you say it?' said Fanny, impatiently.

Mr Sparkler came across the room and stood by his wife's side.

'You make my head ache, Edmund,' said Fanny. 'You look so annoyingly large. Do sit down.'

'Certainly, my dear,' said Mr Sparkler, and sat down.

'This day feels like the longest day ever,' said Fanny, yawning. 'I've never experienced such a long day. Edmund, we must not be alone any more. I really cannot, and will not, have another day like this.'

'No, dear,' said Mr Sparkler. 'But of course, once your brother is better, you will soon have your sister Amy...'

'Dearest Amy, yes!' cried Fanny. 'Poor little Amy will no

doubt have felt Father's loss deeply. I have felt it myself, terribly, of course, but she was with him to the end, which I, unhappily, was not. Dear, dear Father! What a gentleman he was!' There was a long, low knock on the door downstairs, and a few moments later, a servant brought Mr Merdle into the room.

'I was out for a walk, and I thought I'd visit you,' he said, passing his hand over his yellow forehead. 'I was going out to dinner with Mrs Merdle, but I didn't want to eat, so Mrs Merdle went on in the coach.' He sat down on the chair which Mr Sparkler had offered him.

'Thank you,' said Fanny. 'You don't often visit people. You're too busy for that. But you must eat; you must not be ill!'

'Oh! I'm as well as I usually am,' replied Mr Merdle, and then became silent again.

'I was just speaking about poor Father,' began Fanny. She felt she had to continue the conversation. 'My brother has been ill, and that has delayed arranging Father's fortune.'

'Yes, yes,' said Mr Merdle. 'There has been a delay.' He looked exhausted. He passed his hand over his head again.

'Will you meet Mrs Merdle and take the coach home?' asked Fanny. Conversation with Mr Merdle was so difficult!

'No,' he answered. 'I shall walk home, and leave Mrs Merdle to take care of herself.' He looked closely at his hands.

There was then a long silence. Fanny, lying on her sofa, shut her eyes.

'I thought I'd visit you,' said Mr Merdle.

'Thank you,' said Fanny, weakly.

'However, I shall go now,' said Mr Merdle, getting up. 'Could you lend me a penknife?'

Fanny smiled. 'How strange! You're a man of business, Mr Merdle. You must have a knife to open all your letters!'

'I shall go now,' said Mr Merdle, getting up.
'Could you lend me a penknife?'

'Yes,' agreed Mr Merdle. 'You shall have it back tomorrow.'

'Edmund,' said Fanny, 'open the wooden box on my little table, and give Mr Merdle the tortoiseshell penknife.'

Mr Sparkler opened the box and gave Mr Merdle the penknife. The famous visitor shook hands gently with Mrs Sparkler, and went out of the room with Mr Sparkler. After a moment, Mrs Sparkler got up and went to the window for a breath of air. She was sure that it was the longest day ever, and she was tired of fools. Tears of annoyance filled her eyes, as she watched the great Mr Merdle walk away down the street.

The news that Mr Merdle was dead spread through London with surprising speed. At first, he was dead of all the diseases that had ever been known. He had had a problem with his heart, some said, or water on his chest, others thought. But by lunchtime, people were whispering all over London that Mr Merdle had killed himself. Soon, everybody knew that he had been found at the public baths shortly before midnight the night before, a tortoiseshell penknife by his side.

As the day passed, the talk changed again. Mr Merdle had never had any money of his own; he had spent other people's money – lots of it, and without any care! By evening, everyone knew that the great Mr Merdle had been a thief. The man who had been honoured by the great, who had advised government officials, who had been invited to important dinners, respected by all society, was simply the greatest thief who had ever cheated the nation.

The next morning, Pancks rushed into Arthur's office. The talk of the day before had become public: Mr Merdle's bank was broken. The usual work of Arthur's office had stopped.

Arthur sat with his arms on the desk, his head buried in his hands.

Pancks stood at the door of the office. 'I persuaded you to do it, Mr Clennam,' he said at last. 'I know it. Say anything you want. You can't say more than I'm thinking myself.'

'Oh, Pancks, Pancks!' said Arthur. 'I have ruined Doyce! That honest, tireless man, who has worked hard all his life; the man who in spite of so much disappointment has kept such a good and hopeful nature; the man who trusted me to be his partner. I intended to be so true and useful to him. I have ruined him!'

Pancks held his head in his hands, and started tearing at his hair in a cruel manner. 'Blame me!' he cried. 'Say, "You fool, you criminal!"'

'If we had never talked about Mr Merdle, it would have been so much better for you, Pancks, and so much better for me.'

'Mr Clennam, did you put *everything* into Merdle's bank?'

'Everything,' said Clennam, wiping away the tears that had been silently dropping down his face. 'I must give up the management of the business. I must save Doyce's name. The sooner the business goes out of my hands, the better. I must keep nothing for myself. I must work to pay him back as much as I can, for the rest of my life.'

'Is it not possible, sir, to wait for a while and see if things get better?' asked Pancks.

'Impossible, Pancks,' said Arthur. 'All last night I thought about what I would do, and now I just have to do it.'

'I have a friend who is a lawyer, Mr Clennam. May I fetch him for you?'

'If you can spare the time, Pancks, I would be most grateful.'

With the help of Pancks's lawyer friend, Arthur wrote to all his creditors, informing them that his partner was innocent and that he, Arthur, was wholly to blame for what had happened. He gave his small private savings to pay some of the debts. But a few days later, the creditors' lawyers came to Arthur's office to take him to the debtors' prison.

'Now, you know what the Marshalsea is,' said his lawyer. 'Small rooms. Very crowded. You'd be much better in the King's Bench.'

'I would rather go to the Marshalsea,' said Arthur, 'than to any other prison.'

When their coach arrived outside the high walls of the Marshalsea, Mr Chivery was waiting at the gate, and Young John, too. They were astonished to see who the new prisoner was.

'I don't remember, sir, that I was ever less glad to see you,' said Mr Chivery, shaking hands with Arthur.

Arthur sat in the jailers' room by the gate, his eyes fixed on the floor, until Young John touched him on the shoulder and said, 'You can come now.'

Arthur got up and followed Young John, through the old door, up the old stairs, and into the old room.

'I thought you'd like this room, so here it is for you,' said Young John, and he turned and left.

When he was gone, Arthur thought of the good, gentle creature who had spent so much time in this room. He wished with all his heart that he could see her face, full of love and truth. He turned against the wall, and as the tears rolled down his face, he cried, 'Oh, my Little Dorrit!'

— CHAPTER SIX —

A New Prisoner

The day was sunny, and the Marshalsea, with the hot sun shining on it, was unusually quiet. Arthur dropped into the only armchair in the room, and sat thinking. In the unnatural peace of the prison, his thoughts returned constantly to Little Dorrit, and how much the dear creature had influenced his better decisions.

The door opened, and Mr Chivery came in.

'Excuse me for opening the door, sir, but I couldn't make you hear.'

'Did you knock?' said Arthur.

'Six times or more.'

Looking up, Arthur realized that it was late in the afternoon. He had been thinking for hours.

'Your things have come,' said Mr Chivery. 'Young John will bring them up for you now. Can I do anything for you?'

'Many thanks. Nothing.'

Mr Chivery went out and shut the door, and ten minutes later his son carried Arthur's box of personal things into his room.

'Thank you,' said Arthur. 'It's very kind of you.'

He put out his hand, but Young John moved away.

'I don't think I can shake your hand,' he said. 'No; I find I can't!'

Arthur looked at him, puzzled. 'Why are you angry with me?' he said. 'If I've done anything to offend you, I'm sorry.'

'I'd rather not talk about it, sir,' said Young John. But after a moment, he said softly, 'The furniture in this room belongs to me. You're welcome to it. And that little round table belonged to the great gentleman who recently died.'

They were both silent. It was Young John again who spoke. 'How long do you intend to go without food and drink, sir?'

'I'm not hungry just now,' replied Arthur.

'The more reason you should eat, sir,' said John. 'I'm going to have tea in my room. Please come and drink a cup with me.'

Arthur stood up and followed Young John to his room. It was Little Dorrit's old room, now repainted, and more comfortably furnished, but Arthur remembered it clearly from that day when the Dorrits had left the prison forever, and he had lifted her unconscious body from the floor. Young John looked hard at Arthur. 'I see you remember the room, Mr Clennam?'

'I remember it well.'

Young John began to make tea, while Arthur stood at the window. The room spoke to him so sadly of Little Dorrit. He laid his hand on the wall gently, and imagined that he touched her; he spoke her name in a low voice. He looked out of the window at the spikes on the walls, and imagined her in that distant land where she was rich and successful.

Young John put bread, butter, cold meat, and fresh vegetables on the table, and poured the tea. Arthur tried to eat, but the meat sickened him and the bread seemed to turn to sand in his mouth. He could only drink a cup of tea.

Young John watched him. 'Why not take care of yourself?'

'Truly,' said Arthur with a sad smile, 'I have no one to take care of myself for.'

'Well, sir,' said Young John hotly. 'I am surprised that an honest gentleman can give me an answer like that. Really and truly, I am surprised!'

Young John stood up, and then sat down again, never taking his eyes off Arthur.

'Why did I get you the room that you'd like best? Why did I give you my furniture? Why did I carry up your things? Not because of your own goodness, no, but because of someone else's goodness.'

'What is this, John? What can you mean?' cried Arthur. 'I tell you, I do not understand.'

Young John stood staring angrily at Arthur for a moment. Then, slowly, his disbelieving face softened into a face of doubt.

'Mr Clennam,' he said, looking at Arthur thoughtfully, 'do you mean that you don't know?'

'What, John?'

Young John stood up and went over to the window.

'This room, this window, that wall have all been witnesses of it, from day to day, week to week, month to month.'

'Witnesses of what?' said Arthur.

'Of Miss Dorrit's love.'

'For whom?'

'You,' said Young John. And he touched Arthur lightly on the shoulder and then sat down again, with a pale face, shaking his head.

Arthur was shocked. He looked at Young John and his hands dropped at his sides: his whole appearance was of a man who has been woken from sleep.

'Me?' he said at last, trying to smile. 'You're completely mistaken.'

'Ah!' gasped Young John. 'I, mistaken, sir? No, Mr Clennam, don't tell me that. It's nearly killed me with pain. Don't tell me that I'm mistaken.' He wiped his eyes, as tears rolled down his face.

Arthur could not speak. At last, he went slowly back to his room, and sat down in the old armchair, putting his head between his hands. Little Dorrit loved him! Dear Little Dorrit! He had always called her 'child', and had told her that he felt he was getting old. But perhaps she had not thought of him as old. Was there something on his own side that he had quietened as it rose in him? He took out her letter from his box and read it again. He seemed to hear her voice in the words.

Had he whispered to himself that he must not think of her loving him; that he must remember that the time had passed him by, and he was too saddened and old?

Looking back at his own poor story, he saw that Little Dorrit was the centre of his every interest. When she had left England, everything that was good and pleasant in his life had gone, and beyond there was nothing but a darkened sky. He thought of this as he lay down to sleep inside the grey walls of the Marshalsea, and all night the thoughts went around his head.

Little Dorrit was in Arthur's mind constantly after this, but he was not strong enough to guard against misery. He stayed inside his room and was too depressed to make friends with the other prisoners, who did not trust him. Night after night, unable to sleep, he sat at his window, watching the lamps in the yard and looking upwards for the first sight of day. A burning restlessness built up inside him, and a belief that he was going to break his own heart and die in prison. He hated the prison so much that sometimes he could hardly breathe, and he stood at the window, gasping. After a few weeks, he developed a low, slow fever. He was responsible for the failure of Doyce's business, and memories of his foolishness never left his mind.

Mr Plornish visited him, with a basket of food, but Arthur

did not want to see him, and wrote to ask him not to come again. Young John looked in every day, but Arthur always pretended to be busy writing.

On a hot, misty morning, Arthur watched the night end, listening to the rain falling on the yard with an aching head and a tired heart. He felt so ill that he had to rest many times as he washed himself and got back to his chair by the open window. He sat, half sleeping and dreaming. He heard music and songs, which he knew were not real. He began to sleep an exhausted sleep, and he heard voices, and answered them. Then he began to dream of a garden of flowers, in a soft, warm wind.

Painfully, he lifted his head and saw some wonderful flowers by the teacup on his table: a handful of the most lovely flowers. Nothing had ever appeared so beautiful to him. He took them up and smelled them, and lifted them to his hot head. He wondered who had sent them. He tried to drink some tea, but the smell of it was horrible.

He began to dream again, and in his dream, music was playing softly, and the door of his room seemed to open to a light touch. After a moment's pause, a quiet figure seemed to stand there, with a black cloak. It seemed to drop the cloak on the floor, and then it seemed to be his Little Dorrit in her old, shabby dress. It seemed to tremble, and to smile, and then to burst into tears.

He tried to wake up properly, and cried out. And then she came towards him, and with her tears dropping on him as the rain had dropped upon the flowers, Little Dorrit knelt on the floor beside his chair.

*In Arthur's dream, music was playing softly,
and the door of his room seemed to open to a light touch.*

'Oh, my best friend! Dear Mr Clennam! I have come back!'

So gentle and true, and unchanged by fortune!

'They never told me you were ill,' she said.

Little Dorrit put a hand upon his head, and nursed him as she had nursed her father when she was just a child.

When Arthur could speak, he said, 'You have really come to me? And in this dress?'

'I hoped you would like me better in this dress. I've always kept it near me to remind me,' she said softly. 'It was only yesterday evening that I came to London with my brother. Then I heard that you were here. I was thinking of you so anxiously, and it seemed so long until morning. Did you think of me a little?'

'I have thought of you, Little Dorrit, every day, every hour, every minute, since I have been here.'

'Have you? Have you?'

He saw the bright delight of her face, and he felt ashamed. He, a broken, poor, sick prisoner.

Little Dorrit unpacked a basket that she had brought with her. There were cool drinks, pieces of chicken, and fruit. Then she sat next to him, sewing a curtain for his window. She often looked up at him, as he lay back in his chair watching her. Words could not express how dearly he loved her now. She would not let him speak, but now and again she got up to give him a drink.

The sun went down, and she was still there. She finished her work, and put her hand on the arm of his chair.

'Dear Mr Clennam, I must say something to you before I go. I am not going abroad again. My brother has come home with me to see my dear father's lawyers and bankers. I shall be rich, but I have no use for money; I have no wish for it. Will you let me give you all I have? I've never forgotten your kindness to me when this prison was my home. Dear Mr Clennam, make me happy and let me help you!'

He softly answered her. 'No, dear Little Dorrit. I must not hear of such an idea. I can never accept it. I will never touch your fortune, never! I am not desperate enough to carry you – so generous, so good – down with me.'

The bell began to ring, warning visitors to leave.

'One other word, my Little Dorrit. A hard one to me, but it is a necessary one. The time when you belonged to this prison has long gone by.'

'Oh, don't tell me that I must not come back any more!' she cried.

'I am not brave enough to say that. But do not come again soon, do not come often. You belong to much brighter and better places.'

Little Dorrit left Arthur and slowly crossed the yard. The gate shut heavily and hopelessly behind her.

At midnight, Young John came to see Arthur.

'I walked Miss Dorrit to her hotel, sir,' he said.

'Thank you, thank you!'

'She gave me a message for you.' Young John hesitated, and took a deep breath.

'"Promise to take care of him, when I'm not there. Tell him that I send him my undying love." That's what she said. There's my hand, sir, and I'll stand by you forever!'

— CHAPTER SEVEN —
Unfinished Business

One evening, when the sun was low, Rigaud turned in at the gate of the old house and knocked loudly at the door. Mr Flintwinch opened the door and the two men went upstairs to Mrs Clennam's quiet room. The window was wide open and Affery sat near it, sewing.

'Affery, my woman,' said Mr Flintwinch, 'take yourself away!'

Affery threw her sewing down and stood up. 'No, I won't! I'll stay here, and hear everything. I will.'

Mr Flintwinch, stiffening with anger and astonishment, began to move across the room towards her.

'Don't come near me!' cried Affery. 'I'll throw myself out of the window! I'll scream!'

'Stop!' said Mrs Clennam, but Mr Flintwinch had stopped already. 'Leave her alone. Affery, do you turn against me after these many years?'

'I do, yes. I will stay to hear what I don't know. I turn against both of you, and I won't be frightened any more, I won't! I'm here to serve Mr Clennam when he has nothing left, and is ill and in prison and can't be here.'

After looking at her in silence, Mrs Clennam turned to Rigaud. 'You see and hear this foolish creature. Do you mind if she remains here?'

'I, madam? Do I? That's a question for you.'

'I do not,' she said.

Rigaud sat on the table and stretched his legs. He looked

at Mrs Clennam, with his moustache going up and his nose coming down.

'Madam,' he began. 'We have a little business to finish. You must understand first that I am a gentleman who enjoys money. You follow me?'

'Yes,' said Mrs Clennam.

'I am the softest and sweetest of gentlemen, but when people try to play games with me, I become terribly angry. And when that happens, feeding my anger is as important to me as money. Now, let me remind you about our first two meetings.'

'It is not necessary,' said Mrs Clennam.

'Ah, but I want to. And it clears the way. The first time I came here, I was able to look at one or two things in the house. They proved to me that I had found the lady I was looking for. I told our dear Mr Flintwinch that I would return. And return I did. The second time, I told you that I had something to sell, which, if not bought, would put madam in a difficult position. I asked for, I think, one thousand pounds. Will you correct me?'

Forced to speak, she replied, 'You asked for one thousand pounds.'

'Now I ask for two. That is the problem with delaying. So now, madam, I am here for the last time. The last!'

'I tell you again, as I told you before, that we are not rich here, as you suppose,' said Mrs Clennam. 'You told me that you have some papers, and I wish to get those papers back from you. The papers might be worth some money to me.'

'How much, then, madam? Tell me!' He turned on her suddenly with a threatening movement of his hand, seeming to want to hit her.

'I cannot say how much they are worth until I know exactly what they are.'

'You have no fear!' said Rigaud.

'I am very determined,' Mrs Clennam replied.

Rigaud got off the table and sat down near her sofa. 'Let me tell you a little family history, then. A history of a strange marriage, and a strange mother, and of revenge. Yes, yes? I think your heart is beating a little faster, madam... So let me begin this little history. An uncle and his nephew live here, in this house. The uncle is a strong-minded old gentleman; the nephew is shy and frightened.'

Affery was trembling from head to foot. 'Yes, that's Arthur's father and his uncle!' she cried out. 'Arthur's father couldn't even choose his own wife – his uncle chose her!'

Rigaud nodded his head at Affery. 'Perfectly right, Mrs Flintwinch. The uncle tells the nephew to marry. He finds for him a determined lady, a strong lady; a lady without love, cold as stone.'

Mrs Clennam's face had changed, and there was an extraordinary colour in it.

'Madam, I see that I interest you. Let us go on! The nephew does as he is told. But one day the lady discovers a terrible secret about her husband. Full of anger, full of jealousy, she plans her revenge. Because the secret is that her husband has—'

Mrs Clennam was breathing harder, and her lips were trembling.

'Her husband has—' Rigaud went on. 'What does her husband have? Say, then, madam!'

The frozen expression of Mrs Clennam's face was suddenly torn away. She burst out, 'I will tell it myself! I will not hear it from your lips. Since it must be seen, let it be seen by the light I stood in.'

Rigaud pushed his chair back and sat listening to her.

*'I think your heart is beating a little faster, madam...
So let me begin this history.'*

'You don't know what it is to be a child in a house without love,' she said. 'My childhood was one of fear and punishment. I was taught to have a terror of doing wrong. My father wanted me to marry my husband because he was a serious, hard-working young man. I agreed, because I always obeyed my father. But after a year, I discovered that my husband had been secretly married to another woman and had a child with her. He loved a young girl, a poor singer.' Mrs Clennam put her hand on the watch on her table. '*Do Not Forget*. Those were the words of that other woman. She gave this watch to my husband when they separated.'

More than forty years had passed over the grey head of Mrs Clennam since the time she was remembering. Forty years of suffering and anger.

'I forced my husband to tell me the woman's name and address, and I went to see her. I accused her, and she fell at my feet, hiding her face,' Mrs Clennam went on, burning with anger. 'She told me how young she was, how difficult my husband's life had been, and how ashamed they both were. And what did I ask? What was the punishment I asked from her? "You have a child; I have none. You love that child; give him to me. He will believe that he is my son, and everyone will believe that he is mine. His father will promise never to see you again, and you will promise never to communicate with either him or your son." That was all.'

She picked up the watch from the table, opened it, and looked at the letters inside.

'They did not forget. If Arthur was a daily reminder to his father, and if Arthur's absence was a daily pain to his mother, that was only fair. I raised her lost, trembling boy in fear, and he paid the price for the wrongs that were heavy on his head before he was even born. When Arthur's father died, he sent this watch back to me, with its *Do Not Forget*.'

Rigaud shook his head impatiently. 'Come, madam. Come to the stolen money! Come straight to the stolen money, or I will!'

'It was not for the money, you fool.' Mrs Clennam moved in her chair, and almost tried to stand up. 'At the end of his life, my husband's uncle, in a moment of weakness, wrote a new will leaving some money to Arthur's mother.'

Rigaud clapped his hands in her face. 'One thousand pounds was supposed to go to Arthur's mother,' he said. 'Or, if she was dead, one thousand pounds to the daughter of her patron, or, if he had none, to the youngest niece of her patron. And that patron was Mr Frederick Dorrit!'

'That Frederick Dorrit!' said Mrs Clennam. 'He kept a house for singers and players, when he was young and healthy. He raised that poor girl, because she could sing, and then Arthur's father met her. So yes, I kept that new will a secret, and kept it here with me in this house, for many years. I did not bring it to light because it rewarded wrong-doing. It was a moment of madness by my husband's uncle. When the will was at last destroyed – as I thought – Frederick Dorrit had long been ruined. He had no daughter. I had found the youngest niece, Little Dorrit, and what I did for her was much better than money.'

'And now I have the will,' said Rigaud.

Mrs Clennam and Mr Flintwinch stared at each other. At last, still staring at her, old Mr Flintwinch spoke.

'When you told me about that will, I advised you to destroy it, but no, you wanted to keep it. You hid that paper away until we were expecting Arthur home any day. He had not been back in this room ten minutes, when he spoke of his father's watch. So I put the will in a box, locked it, and gave it to my brother, who came here that night on his way to Antwerp. The next day, you asked me to burn it, but my brother had already taken it with him.'

'Where I met him!' laughed Rigaud. 'So tired after his long journey that he slept like a baby and never even noticed when I took the paper from him!'

Mrs Clennam dropped her head in her hand. Her other hand pushed hard on the table, and again she seemed almost ready to stand up.

'I do not have two thousand pounds to give you now,' she said to Rigaud. 'What will you take for your silence?'

'My sweet lady,' said Rigaud. 'I have given a copy of the will to another. If you delay until the Marshalsea gate is shut tonight, your son Arthur will have read it.'

She put her two hands to her head, let out a loud cry, and pulled herself to her feet. For a moment, her body shook, but then she stood strong.

'Say what you mean! Say what you mean, man!'

'Before I came here tonight, I gave a copy of the will to Miss Dorrit, the little niece of Mr Frederick, who I met abroad. Unless someone takes it back before the Marshalsea bell rings tonight, she will give it to your son!'

Nearly falling again, Mrs Clennam ran to a cupboard, violently pulled the door open, and took out a cloak. Affery, who had watched her in terror, ran to the middle of the room and caught hold of her dress.

'Don't, don't! Where are you going? I'll keep your secret. Don't go out; you'll fall dead in the street. Tell me where you've kept Arthur's poor mother, and I'll nurse her.'

Mrs Clennam looked at Affery in astonishment. 'Kept her?' she said. 'She's been dead for twenty years! Ask Flintwinch – he'll tell you that she died when Arthur went abroad.'

Affery trembled. 'What is it in the house, then? What is it that makes the noises and shakes the dust?'

Mrs Clennam did not listen to her. 'Wait here until I come back!' she said to Rigaud, and ran out of the house and then wildly through the gate and into the street.

For a moment, the others stood still. Affery was the first to move. She ran downstairs and outside, following Mrs Clennam. Next, Mr Flintwinch went slowly to the door, in his sideways manner, without a word.

Rigaud was left alone. He sat by the window. 'You will get your money,' he said to himself. 'You have lived a gentleman; you will die a gentleman.'

— CHAPTER EIGHT —

Sunshine and Shade

The summer sun was going down behind the houses and the streets were beginning to darken as a woman dressed in black, and with a pale, wild face, walked through the streets. She moved rapidly, but was weak and uncertain. People stopped to look at her as she rushed by. She crossed the bridge, and arrived at last at the gate of the Marshalsea.

'I would like to see Miss Dorrit. Is she here?'

'Yes, she is,' said Mr Chivery. 'Can I ask your name, madam?'

'Mrs Clennam.'

'Mr Clennam's mother?' he asked.

She hesitated, then nodded, and he took her upstairs to a room where she could wait. The room looked down into the darkening yard, where prisoners were walking slowly around, talking to friends. The air was heavy and hot, and from outside there was a rush of sounds. Mrs Clennam stood at the window until she heard a soft word of surprise, and Little Dorrit stood before her.

'Is it possible, Mrs Clennam? You are better—' said Little Dorrit. Then she stopped, for there was neither happiness nor health in the face that turned to her.

'I've come to collect some papers that were left with you,' said Mrs Clennam, anxiously.

Little Dorrit took out the packet.

'Have you read the papers inside?'

Frightened by her being there, like a picture that had come

to life, Little Dorrit answered, 'No.'

'Read them.'

Little Dorrit opened the packet, and stood by the window to read the papers, crying out a few times in terror and astonishment. When she had finished, she looked around at Mrs Clennam.

'You know now what I have done,' said Mrs Clennam.

'I think so. I'm afraid so. But I feel so sorry, and so full of pity, that I can't follow all I've read,' said Little Dorrit, trembling.

'I will give back what I owe you. Forgive me. Can you forgive me?' Mrs Clennam knelt down.

'I can, and I do! I forgive you freely. Please get up; you are too old to kneel. Let me help you.' Little Dorrit took Mrs Clennam's hands and helped her to stand.

'I have something to ask,' said Mrs Clennam. 'I beg you not to tell Arthur about this until I am dead.'

'I'm so sorry and my thoughts are confused,' said Little Dorrit. 'But if I am sure that knowing this will do Mr Clennam no good, I will not tell him.'

'Thank you!' Mrs Clennam stood in the shadow, so Little Dorrit could not see her face, but her voice was strong and broken at the same time.

'You will wonder, perhaps, why I am telling you this, and not him. I was always hard with Arthur. He never loved me, but he always respected me. I don't want to lose his respect, while I'm alive.' Her pride was very strong, and the pain of it was sharp when she spoke.

The first warning bell began to ring in the yard below.

'I have something else to ask you!' cried Mrs Clennam. 'The man who brought you this packet is waiting at my house. He has threatened that you will tell Arthur everything if I don't pay him, but I do not have enough money. Will you come and tell him that you already know the truth?'

Little Dorrit agreed, and they left the prison together. It was a long, light summer evening and the sky was calm and beautiful. People sat at their doors, playing with their children and enjoying the air. They had arrived near the gate of Mrs Clennam's house when there was a sudden noise like thunder.

'What was that?' cried Mrs Clennam. 'Let's hurry in.'

But Little Dorrit, with a sharp cry, held her back.

In one quick moment, they saw the old house in front of them, with Rigaud sitting at the open window upstairs. Another thundering sound, and the house moved, opened apart in fifty places, and fell slowly into ruins, as they watched. Deafened by the noise, covered with the dust, they hid their faces in terror, and stood unable to move.

Then, they ran back from the gate and towards the main road, crying and shouting. There, Mrs Clennam dropped to the ground; and from that hour, she never moved a finger again, or spoke a single word for the rest of her life. Affery had been looking for them at the prison, and she came up now to help Mrs Clennam into a neighbour's house, and to look after her. Affery had been right about her facts, and wrong about the reasons for them. The noises in the old house had been the sounds of the building weakening for years, and finally it had fallen. When the great storm of dust cleared, and the summer night was calm again, people came to dig through the ruins.

Rigaud had been killed by the falling bricks and wood. But Mr Flintwinch was never found. Perhaps he had left the house before it fell. Perhaps he had taken as much money as he could find and escaped from London. Perhaps the reports that were heard many times of a bent, old Englishman living in Amsterdam, who walked sideways and looked very like Mr Flintwinch, were really true.

Another thundering sound, and the house moved, opened apart in fifty places, and fell slowly into ruins.

Arthur continued to lie very ill in the Marshalsea. Little Dorrit was there every day, thinking for him, working for him, and watching him. Outside the Marshalsea, she was looking after others, too: Fanny, who always wanted comfort but was determined not to be comforted; and her brother Edward, who was weak and proud and could do nothing for himself.

But at last, slowly, the Marshalsea prisoner's health began to return. One fresh autumn day, he sat weakly, listening to a voice that read to him. Outside the prison, the golden fields had been cut and the apples were shining red among the yellowing leaves. The Marshalsea, unchanging and hard, had not a touch of these beautiful colours and richness on it. But Arthur, listening to Little Dorrit, heard in her gentle voice everything that nature was doing beyond the stones and bars of the prison.

When she stopped reading, Little Dorrit brought her chair closer to his side.

'Have you been here many times when I have not seen you, Little Dorrit?' he asked.

'Yes, I have been here very often,' she replied.

'Every day?'

'I think,' said Little Dorrit after hesitating, 'that I have been here at least twice every day.'

'Dear Little Dorrit, we must learn to say goodbye again. You must stop coming here and go back to your own life. We must follow our different paths which lead so far apart. You haven't forgotten what we said together when you came back?'

'Oh no, I haven't forgotten! But something has—' she hesitated. 'You feel quite strong today, don't you? Do you feel strong enough to know what a great fortune I've got?'

'I shall be very glad to know. No fortune can be too great for Little Dorrit.'

'I've been so wanting to tell you.' She looked at him silently. There was something happy and proud in her face, but he thought she might break into tears in a moment. 'I must tell you about Fanny first,' she said. 'You will be sorry to hear that poor Fanny has lost everything. She has nothing left but her husband's income. All the money that Father gave her was in Mr Merdle's bank, and it has all gone.'

Arthur was more sad than surprised. 'I had feared so, because of the connection between her husband and Mr Merdle.'

'Yes, I am very sorry for poor Fanny. My poor brother, too, has lost his money in the same way. But how much do you think my own great fortune is?'

She paused, and Arthur felt suddenly anxious.

'I have nothing in the world! I am as poor as when I lived here! Father put all his money in Mr Merdle's bank, and it has all gone. Now, my dearest Arthur, you can share my fortune.' She looked up at him, and she felt his tears on her face. 'We shall never say goodbye again! I never was rich before, I never was proud before, I never was happy. I would rather spend my life here with you, than have the greatest fortune ever. I love you dearly! I wish Father could know my happiness, in this room where he suffered for so many years.'

The autumn days went on. One morning, as Arthur listened for Little Dorrit's light feet, he heard her coming, but not alone.

'Dear Arthur,' said her happy voice outside the door. 'You have a visitor. May I bring someone in?'

And there was Mr Meagles, cheerful and sun-browned. He

put his arms around Arthur, like a father.

'Arthur, my dear man,' said Mr Meagles, 'Miss Dorrit wrote to me as soon as she had seen you for the first time, but I could not come until I had found Doyce.'

'Poor Doyce!' sighed Arthur.

'He's not poor; he's doing well. Doyce has been very successful abroad. He's fallen on his feet. I tell you, you wouldn't believe it if you saw the wonderful things he's doing over there. He doesn't need the Circumlocution Office any more, he has managed without them!'

'What a load you take from my mind!' cried Arthur. 'What happiness you give me!'

'Happiness!' replied Mr Meagles. 'Don't talk about happiness until you see Daniel Doyce. I went and found him out there, and so we came back together.'

'Doyce in England?' gasped Arthur.

'We're both in England – and here he is!' said Mr Meagles, throwing open his arms.

Doyce ran in from behind the door and caught Arthur with both hands.

'I have two things to say, my dear Clennam,' said Doyce. 'First, not a word more from you about the past. You made a mistake, and you will learn from the failure. Every failure teaches a man something, and you are too sensible a man not to learn from this one. Secondly, I'm sorry that you felt your mistake so painfully. I've been travelling day and night to get home. Mr Meagles and I put the business right again, and it needs you more than ever. My dear Clennam, your old office is waiting for you. There is nothing to keep you here half an hour longer!'

There was silence, which was not broken until Arthur had

stood for some time at the window, and Little Dorrit had gone to him.

'I can see that I made a mistake when I said that there is nothing to keep you here half an hour longer,' said Doyce then. 'Am I right in thinking that we need to organize a wedding?'

'You are,' said Arthur.

And so the day ended, and then the night, and the morning came, and Little Dorrit, in a simple dress, came into the prison with the sunshine. The poor prison room was a happy place that morning. Where in the world was there a room so full of quiet happiness?

And so, in front of Mr Plornish, Mr Pancks, Mr and Mrs Meagles and their daughter Pet, Daniel Doyce, John Chivery and Mr Chivery, and all the jailers from the Marshalsea, Amy and Arthur were married, with the sun shining on them.

Afterwards, they paused for a moment, looking along the street in the autumn morning sunshine. Then they went down the steps into a quiet life of usefulness and happiness, to give a mother's care, in time, to Fanny's children – and to their own, too – while that lady went into society every day. They went down to be a nurse and friend to Tip, who was never ashamed of the great demands he made on his sister. They went quietly down to move along the noisy streets, happy and inseparable, through sunshine and shade.

GLOSSARY

admire *(v)* to think or say that somebody or something is very good; **admiringly** *(adv)*
admirer *(n)* a person who admires somebody or something
apron *(n)* something that you wear over the front of your clothes to keep them clean, especially when you are cooking
astonished *(adj)* very surprised
astonishment *(n)* a feeling of great surprise
candle *(n)* a round stick of wax, solid oil, or fat with a piece of string in the middle that burns to give light
cap *(n)* a soft hat with a hard, curved part at the front
cloak *(n)* a long, loose coat without separate sleeves for your arms
coach *(n)* a moving vehicle with four wheels that is pulled by horses
comfort *(n)* a person or thing that helps you or makes life better
creditor *(n)* a person or company from whom you have borrowed money
debt *(n)* money that you must pay back to somebody
debtor *(n)* a person who owes money
department *(n)* one of the parts of a university, school, government, shop, big company, etc.
deserve *(v)* to be good or bad enough to have something
dignity *(n)* calm and serious behaviour that makes other people respect you
faint *(v)* to suddenly become unconscious for a short time, for example because you are weak, ill, or shocked
gallery *(n)* a place where people can look at or buy art
gentleman *(n)* a man who is polite and kind to other people
gentlemanly *(adj)* behaving very well; like a gentleman

gondola *(n)* a long boat with a flat bottom and high parts at each end, used on canals in Venice, Italy

gondolier *(n)* a person whose job is to guide and move a gondola

gown *(n)* a long, loose piece of clothing

heir *(n)* a person who gets money, a house, etc. when someone dies

honour *(n)* something that makes you proud and pleased; *(v)* to show that you respect somebody or something

honourable *(adj)* behaving in a way that makes people respect you

inherit *(v)* to get money or things from somebody who has died

insult *(v)* to be deliberately rude to somebody

jailer *(n)* a person whose job is to guard prisoners

nod *(v)* to move your head down and up again quickly, usually because you agree with or understand something

partner *(n)* one of the people who owns a business

patron *(n)* a person who gives money and support to artists, writers, and musicians

penknife *(n)* a small knife that you can carry in your pocket

poverty *(n)* the situation of being poor

pride *(n)* the feeling that you are happy with something that you have got or have done

puff *(v)* to breathe quickly or loudly

quarantine *(n)* The time when a person who may have a disease must be kept away from other people. In the nineteenth century, quarantine was often used when people travelled from one country to another, to control the spread of disease.

release *(v)* to let a person or an animal go free

respect *(n & v)* thinking that somebody is very good or clever

respectful *(adj)* If you are respectful, you are polite to other people in different situations.

Glossary

reward *(v)* to give something to somebody because they have done something well or worked hard

riches *(n)* a lot of money and valuable things

shabby *(adj)* old and untidy or dirty because it has been used a lot

sigh *(v)* to let out a deep breath, for example because you are sad

smart *(adj)* clean and tidy

smarten (up) *(v)* to make yourself, somebody, or something look tidy and nicer

spike *(n)* a piece of metal with a sharp point

strike *(v)* When a clock strikes, it rings a bell a certain number of times so that people know what time it is. (past tense **struck**)

tortoiseshell *(adj)* made from a hard material that is usually orange and brown

trust *(v)* to believe that somebody is honest and good

will *(n)* a piece of paper that says who will have your money, house, etc. when you die

wipe *(v)* to make something clean or dry with a cloth

yard *(n)* an area next to a building, usually with a wall around it

STORY NOTES

Amsterdam   the capital city of the Netherlands
Antwerp   a city in the north of Belgium
Calais   an important French port (where ships arrive and leave) for travel to England
the Channel   the sea between England and France
Circumlocution Office   a government department invented by Dickens (circumlocution means using many words to say something simple)
Covent Garden   a place in London with an important market
Dover   an important English port for travel to France
Florence   a famous historical city in Italy
Grand Canal   one of the most important canals in Venice, Italy
Grosvenor Square   a large garden square in London where fashionable people liked to live
Iron Bridge   another name for Southwark Bridge, which crossed the River Thames
King's Bench   a prison where debtors were often kept
London Bridge   a famous bridge over the River Thames between the City of London and Southwark
Marseille   a city on the south (Mediterranean) coast of France, and an important port
Marshalsea Prison   a prison in London, where people were sent when they could not pay their debts
Martigny   a mountain town in Switzerland
Mediterranean   a sea between Europe and North Africa
Putney Heath   a large park where many Londoners came to enjoy the clean air
Twickenham   (in the nineteenth century) a fashionable town on the River Thames near London

ABOUT VICTORIAN LONDON

Under Queen Victoria (1837–1901), London changed very fast. Thousands of people moved there looking for work, because new factories were being built, and railways were developing. The city grew rapidly: there were one million people living there in 1800, but by the end of the century, the population was six million.

These were exciting times, but difficult ones, too. London soon became a noisy, crowded, and horribly dirty place. The streets were filled with people and horses, and the air was foggy with the smoke from fires and factories. Disease was common, and many people died young.

Society
Social class was very important in Victorian times. Working class people did jobs like street-selling or factory work, and they often earned very low wages. The middle classes were

a growing group during this time: they were people who dressed well and did 'clean work' in the many new banks and companies that were starting up. Some of these people were very rich, but the upper classes – aristocrats who did not work and lived off their inherited wealth – still believed that they were the most important people in society. Many of these aristocrats liked to do 'grand tours' of Europe, visiting places like Venice and Rome to see the many artistic and historical sights and to enjoy fashionable society.

Family life

Victorian families were usually large, often with five or six children. All families except those who were poor had servants, and women were expected to look after the home while men went out to work. But many working class women did jobs like sewing or cleaning to increase the family income. Their children often went out to work, too.

Poverty

For poor people, life was terribly hard. Often whole families lived in just one room in a large house with other families. They had nowhere to cook, and no running water, and they had to go to one of the many new public baths to wash.

Anyone who had no job or who was too sick to work was sent to a workhouse. People lived in fear of the workhouse: here they were separated from their families, forced to wear uniforms, and given hard and unpleasant jobs to do.

---

aristocrat *(n)* a member of the highest social class
class *(n)* a group of people who are the same in some way
population *(n)* the number of people who live in a place

ABOUT CHARLES DICKENS

Charles John Huffam Dickens (1812–70) was born in Portsmouth, in the south of England. Dickens spent some happy childhood years in Kent, but when the family moved to London, his father was imprisoned for debt in the Marshalsea prison, and at the age of twelve Dickens was sent to work in a factory. Later, he was able to return to school for a few years, and after working for a time as an office boy, he became a journalist, writing for various newspapers.

In these early years Dickens got to know London extremely well and everything that he had learned about the city became very useful to him when he wrote his novels.

In 1836, he married Catherine Hogarth, and in the same year his first novel, *The Pickwick Papers*, began to appear in a monthly magazine. It was very popular, and was soon followed by *Oliver Twist* and several more novels. They were all written as serials, with one part appearing each month in a magazine, and they were only published as books later. Readers eagerly greeted each new novel, and Dickens quickly became both successful and wealthy.

As he grew older, Dickens worked harder than ever, producing novels like *David Copperfield*, *Bleak House*, and *Great Expectations*, which are among his finest works. Dickens toured Britain and the United States, giving public readings from his works. It was a very full, but also exhausting life, and in 1870, at the age of fifty-eight, Dickens died suddenly, leaving unfinished his last novel, *The Mystery of Edwin Drood*.

Little Dorrit was published between 1855 and 1857, and it is now widely considered as one of Dickens's best works. In Little Dorrit, Dickens wrote about the Marshalsea Prison, of which he had such bitter childhood memories. But he also wrote about some of the things he disliked in society: the over-complicated and inefficient running of government; the unwritten laws that keep people from different social classes apart; and the dishonesty and unhappiness of those who care only for wealth. He had a great interest in the social problems of the times – a concern that appears in many of his novels.

Many books have been written about the life and works of Charles Dickens, and many of his stories have been made into films and stage productions. He is often called the greatest English novelist of all time, and his characters and their sayings have become so real to us that they are now part of our language and our everyday life.

---

novel *(n)* a book that tells a story about things that are not real
publish *(v)* to produce a book, magazine, or newspaper for selling
stage *(n)* the part of a theatre where the actors, dancers, etc. stand in a theatre

ACTIVITIES

Before reading

1 **Look at the front and back cover, and the contents page. Then answer the questions.**

   1 Who wrote *Little Dorrit*?
   2 Does the story happen in our time or in the past?
   3 Who are the two most important characters in the story?
   4 Do you think the story will have a happy or a sad ending?

2 **Match the words with their meanings.**

   poverty   admire   jailer   partner   debt   inherit

   1 Money that you must pay back to someone.
   2 A person who guards prisoners.
   3 Having little or no money.
   4 To get money or things from somebody who has died.
   5 To think or say that somebody is very good.
   6 One of the people who owns a business.

3 **What do you think is going to happen in the story? Choose the correct words to complete the sentences.**

   1 Little Dorrit *goes / does not go* to live with Mrs Clennam.
   2 Little Dorrit becomes Arthur's *friend / wife*.
   3 Little Dorrit becomes very *rich / poor*.
   4 Arthur *goes / does not go* to prison.
   5 Arthur *learns / does not learn* the truth about his mother's secret.

ACTIVITIES

While Reading

Part 1: Poverty

Read Chapter 1. Write the names of the characters.

Affery   Arthur   Mr Meagles   Arthur's father   Mrs Clennam

1 _____ has been abroad for many years.
2 _____ is a happy man with a wife and child.
3 _____ has not left her house for many years.
4 _____ sent his wife something before he died.
5 _____ has worked for Mrs Clennam for many years.

Read Chapter 2. Choose the correct words to complete the sentences.

1 Mr William Dorrit has *two / three* children.
2 Outside the prison, Arthur meets Little Dorrit's *uncle / father*.
3 *Many / No* visitors come to see Mr Dorrit in prison.
4 Arthur gives Mr Dorrit some *clothes / money*.
5 Mr Plornish is the Dorrit family's *friend / debtor*.

Read Chapter 3. Correct the <u>underlined</u> word in each sentence to make the sentences true.

1 Arthur goes to the Circumlocution Office <u>four</u> times.
2 Mr Meagles is in a <u>good</u> temper when he comes out of the Circumlocution Office.
3 Daniel Doyce is an engineer and <u>debtor</u>.
4 <u>Everyone</u> knows how important Doyce's invention is.
5 Arthur wants to pay Little Dorrit's <u>sister's</u> debts.

Read Chapter 4. Are the sentences true or false?

1 Little Dorrit is in love with John Chivery.
2 John Chivery's father is a jailer.
3 Frederick dresses better than his brother.
4 Mr Chivery is usually rude to Mr Dorrit.
5 Mr Dorrit thinks that he is the most important person in the Marshalsea Prison.

Read Chapter 5. Match the parts of the sentences.

1 Arthur   a wants information about the Dorrit family.
2 Doyce   b cannot get back into the house.
3 Pancks   c and Arthur become partners.
4 Mrs Clennam   d brings an important letter from Paris.
5 Affery   e looks at Doyce's papers.
6 Rigaud   f kisses Little Dorrit's forehead.

Read Chapter 6. Choose the correct words to complete the sentences.

1 Pancks has discovered that Mr Dorrit is *rich / ill*.
2 Mr Dorrit has inherited a great *factory / house* in Dorset.
3 When Little Dorrit hears the news at Mr Casby's house, she *faints / cries*.
4 Mr Chivery burns Frederick Dorrit's old *papers / clothes*.
5 A coach arrives at *twelve / eleven* to take the Dorrit family from the prison.

Part 2: Riches

Read Chapter 1. Are the sentences true, false, or not mentioned in the story?

1 Little Dorrit does not like Mr Rigaud.
2 A lady and her son use the Dorrit family's hotel rooms.
3 Mrs Merdle's first husband was from Italy.
4 Little Dorrit feels comfortable in her new life.
5 Mr Sparkler has travelled to many different parts of Italy.
6 Mr Dorrit thinks Little Dorrit should behave differently.

Read Chapter 2. Put the events in order.

a Arthur meets Rigaud at his mother's house.
b Pancks goes to Arthur's home for dinner.
c Doyce goes abroad.
d Affery tells Arthur about strange noises in the house.
e Arthur receives a letter from Little Dorrit.
f Pancks tells Arthur to put his money in Merdle's bank.

Read Chapter 3. Answer the questions.

1 Who visits the Dorrits when they first arrive in Rome?
2 Where is Mr Sparkler's new position?
3 Who gave him the job?
4 When do Fanny and Mr Sparkler get married?
5 Who visits Mr Dorrit at his hotel?
6 What kind of advice does Mr Dorrit want from Mr Merdle?

Read Chapter 4. Then correct the <u>underlined</u> word in each sentence to make the sentences true.

1 Mr Dorrit writes John Chivery a cheque for <u>fifty</u> pounds.
2 Mr Dorrit travels from London to <u>Florence</u>.
3 Mr Dorrit begins to fall <u>down</u> during meals.
4 At Mrs Merdle's he thinks that he is back in the <u>hotel</u>.
5 Little Dorrit cares for her ill <u>brother</u>.
6 After <u>Frederick</u> Dorrit dies, his brother dies too.

Read Chapter 5. Then write the names of the characters.

1 Fanny is tired of _____.
2 _____'s brother is ill.
2 _____ goes to dinner without her husband.
3 _____ wants to borrow a penknife.
5 Arthur has ruined _____.
6 _____ goes to prison.

Read Chapter 6. Are the sentences true or false?

1 John Chivery gives Arthur Little Dorrit's old room in the prison.
2 John refuses to shake Arthur's hand.
3 All the furniture in Arthur's prison room belonged to William Dorrit.
4 John tells Arthur that Little Dorrit was in love with him.
5 Little Dorrit wants to give Arthur her money.

Read Chapter 7. Match the quotes with the people who say them in the story.

1 'Affery, my woman. Take yourself away!'
2 'Don't come near me! I'll throw myself out of the window!'
3 'You see and hear this foolish creature. Do you mind if she remains here?'
4 'You must understand first that I am a gentleman who enjoys money.'
5 'When you told me about that will, I advised you to destroy it.'
6 'Tell me where you've kept Arthur's poor mother, and I'll nurse her.'

a Affery to Mrs Clennam.
b Rigaud to Mrs Clennam.
c Mr Flintwinch to his wife.
d Mr Flintwinch to Mrs Clennam.
e Mrs Clennam to Rigaud.
f Affery to her husband.

Read Chapter 8. Are the sentences true or false?

1 Mrs Clennam comes to the prison because she's better.
2 Little Dorrit can't forgive Mrs Clennam.
3 Arthur doesn't respect his mother.
4 Mrs Clennam dies when her house falls down.
5 Little Dorrit tells Arthur that she has no money.
6 Doyce wants Arthur to work for him again.

ACTIVITIES

After Reading

Vocabulary

1 Match the <u>underlined</u> phrases from the story with the meanings below.

suddenly said   stopped liking   all over
thinking carefully   a lot of

1 'It makes me shake <u>from head to foot</u> when I hear him.'
2 She was standing looking down at the river, <u>deep in thought</u>.
3 He gave them <u>a great deal of</u> advice.
4 The Dorrits had <u>turned against</u> him.
5 She <u>burst out</u>, 'I will tell it myself!'

2 Complete the table with the words below.

hall   candle   gentleman   will   yard   patron
gondola   apron   gallery   gondolier   cap
admirer   prison   jailer   factory

People	Places	Things

Grammar

1 Write the sentences using the past simple or past continuous tense.

1 when / Arthur / first / see / Little Dorrit, she / sew / in his mother's room
2 Amy / bring / Mr Dorrit / his meal / and / he / eat it / quickly
3 Arthur / meet / Mr Meagles / when / he / be / at the Circumlocution Office
4 Tip Dorrit / leave / prison / because / someone / pay / his debts
5 while / he / visit / London, Mr Dorrit / have / dinner with an important banker
6 they / take / Arthur / to prison / because / he / cannot / pay / his debts

2 Complete the paragraph with the relative pronouns *who*, *which*, *where*, *when*, or *whose*.

When Pancks found Arthur in the office ¹_____ he worked, Arthur was very upset. Merdle, ²_____ had been respected by all, was a thief. And the money ³_____ everyone had put in his bank was gone. The man, ⁴_____ friends had trusted him with their fortunes, had cheated them all. And now he was dead. Merdle's body had been found at the public baths ⁵_____ a cleaner came to lock up the building. He had killed himself with a penknife, ⁶_____ they found by his side.

Arthur, ⁷_____ money was in Merdle's bank, put his head in his hands. 'I'm ruined,' he said. 'And so is poor Doyce, ⁸_____ trusted me so much.'

'Blame me!' Pancks cried. 'I am the one ⁹_____ advised you to put all your money into that bank.'

Reading

1 Put these sentences about Arthur Clennam in the order that they happen in the story.

a He follows Little Dorrit.
b He meets Pancks.
c He goes to prison.
d He returns to England.
e He marries Little Dorrit.
f His father dies.
g He waits at the Circumlocution Office.
h He gives Mr Dorrit some money.

2 Read the descriptions. Write two characters for each description. You may use some names more than once.

John Chivery   Arthur Clennam   Mr Clennam
Fanny Dorrit   Little Dorrit   Mr Dorrit   Mr Meagles

In the story, these people...

1 have worked abroad.
2 marry someone they do not love.
3 have spent time in quarantine.
4 love somebody who does not know it.
5 go to prison for their debts.

Writing

1 Read the letter. Then answer the questions.

> *Dear Mr Plornish*
>
> *I have just received a letter from Miss Amy Dorrit, who wishes to be remembered to you. You will be pleased to hear that the Dorrits are in good health, and they have just arrived safely in Venice. Miss Amy Dorrit thinks of you, and she has not forgotten your kindness to her family. However, she asks us not to write to her. I fear that she is the only Dorrit who wishes to remember her past.*
>
> *Regards,*

1 Who wrote the letter? Why?
2 How does the writer feel?

2 You are Mr Plornish. Write a reply to the letter, using these notes.

- You want to thank the sender for his / her letter.
- You are happy that the Dorrits are safe and well.
- You are sorry that you cannot write to Amy Dorrit.
- You hope to see her and the family again one day.

3 Now write one of these letters in your own words.

1 Write a letter from Arthur to his mother. Arthur tells her that his father is dead and says that he is sending his gold watch. He also writes that he is coming home.
2 Write a letter from Rigaud to Mrs Clennam. Rigaud says that he knows a secret about her past, and he wants £1,000 for his silence.

Speaking

1 Who says these sentences?

1 'I wish you hadn't followed me.'
2 'I only wish you had found me in a better temper.'
3 'I've recently stopped working in my mother's business, and now I wish to find a new job.'
4 'I wish you would smarten yourself up a little.'
5 'I wish the boy didn't spend his money on clothes.'
6 'I am sorry that you have not been pleased with me.'
7 'I hope that you sometimes have a thought for me.'
8 'If we had never talked about Mr Merdle, it would have been so much better.'

2 Now use three different colours to underline words and phrases in Exercise 1 which...

- express wishes for the present or future.
- express unhappiness about a present situation.
- express regrets about the past.

3 In pairs, role-play this conversation between Arthur and John Chivery. Use the words and phrases in Exercise 1 to help you.

Arthur...

- regrets putting money into Mr Merdle's bank.
- wishes he was not in prison.
- hopes that he will see Little Dorrit again one day.

John Chivery...

- tells Arthur that Little Dorrit loves him.
- says he will look after Arthur, because of Little Dorrit.

THE OXFORD BOOKWORMS LIBRARY

THE OXFORD BOOKWORMS LIBRARY is a best-selling series of graded readers which provides authentic and enjoyable reading in English. It includes a wide range of original and adapted texts: classic and modern fiction, non-fiction, and plays. There are more than 250 Bookworms to choose from, in seven carefully graded language stages that go from beginner to advanced level.

Each Bookworm is illustrated, and offers extensive support, including:
- a glossary of above-level words
- activities to develop language and communication skills
- notes about the author and story
- online tests

Each Bookworm pack contains a reader and audio.

6	STAGE 6	2500 HEADWORDS	CEFR B2–C1
5	STAGE 5	1800 HEADWORDS	CEFR B2
4	STAGE 4	1400 HEADWORDS	CEFR B1–B2
3	STAGE 3	1000 HEADWORDS	CEFR B1
2	STAGE 2	700 HEADWORDS	CEFR A2–B1
1	STAGE 1	400 HEADWORDS	CEFR A1–A2
S	STARTER	250 HEADWORDS	CEFR A1

Find a full list of *Bookworms* and resources at
www.oup.com/elt/gradedreaders

If you liked this stage 5 Bookworm, why not try...

Great Expectations
CHARLES DICKENS

By Miss Havisham's side sits a beautiful girl, and in front of her, stands young Pip. Miss Havisham stares at Pip coldly, and murmurs to the girl: 'Break his heart, Estella!'